YOU IN ME, FOREVER...

PRABHA KARAN

ISBN
Paperback 978-969-679-263-5

Objective

Have you ever looked into someone's eyes and felt completely understood? Maybe it was a romantic partner, a crush, a close friend, or even a family member. In that moment, the boundary between you seemed to fade away—as if you weren't just connecting with them, but actually recognizing yourself in them.

These moments of deep recognition can feel almost mystical. When we truly identify with another person, we glimpse something profound about the nature of existence itself. It's no coincidence that the greatest spiritual experiences are often described in the same terms as falling in love – a sense of boundaries dissolving, of two becoming one.

But relationships aren't always this beautiful. Sometimes they're confusing, challenging, and even painful. We struggle to understand each other, to maintain connections, to find lasting happiness together. Even when we feel deeply for someone, we might find ourselves acting in ways that create distance rather than closeness.

What if there was a way to understand these experiences—both the transcendent moments of connection and the painful ones of separation? What if the same understanding that helps you be a better partner, friend, or family member could also lead you to profound fulfillment in your own life?

This book hopes to offer timeless wisdom about the nature of human existence, with lessons about finding fulfillment in our lives and in our relationships with those we hold most dear. You'll discover how your Intellect—that remarkable power within your personality that sets humans apart from all other life—can help you transform your connections with others while finding greater happiness yourself.

This practical and profound journey will explore ideas that might challenge your current understanding of yourself and your relationships. But we'll do it step by step, using examples and experiences you'll recognize from your own life.

Whether you're seeking deeper connections with others, greater personal fulfillment, or both, this book will show you how they're intimately linked— and how they always have been and always will be.

Contents

———✦✦———

Contents

Chapter 01

Your Intellect

———◆◆———

Being born as a human is an extremely rare and wonderful opportunity. There are billions of living things here on Earth, from the greatest mammals to the smallest microbes. Adding in plant life, the number of living things becomes so high that it can't even be counted. But within this vast amount of life, there are only 8 billion human beings. This is why we say it is extremely rare to be a human.

In this extraordinary web of life, where every creature is connected to every other in countless ways, humans hold a unique position. What sets us apart from all those other life forms? It's a remarkable quality called **the Intellect**. Understanding the Intellect is the most important part of understanding what makes you who you are. Let's explore this special quality and discover how it shapes not only our individual experience of life but our connection to the vast universe around us—from the Infinite cosmos to the people we hold most dear to us.

The INTELLECT is a powerful mechanism within your personality that manifests in the form of a single precise thought. By using the Intellect, you think, reason, compare, posit, infer, judge, and make decisions logically. No other form of life has this power. If this word is familiar to you, you may think that you already know what it means. In everyday use, the word *Intellect* often means the same thing as *intelligence, the Mind, genius,* or other similar words. But the truth is that it means something very specific in relation to what makes us human—and something beautiful in how it allows us to understand our place in the universe.

We can understand the Intellect better by seeing how it differs from these other similar terms:

- **Intelligence** is nothing but pool of data or information that is available online, books, and in your memory. It is just a set of data that a person is able to draw on when they use their Intellect.

- **The Mind** is the place inside us that contains all of our flowing, unorganized thoughts, seat of our desires and all emotions, both positive and negative. The Intellect is responsible for organizing these thoughts, desires, and emotions and using them to decide which actions to perform.

• A person can be called a **genius** if they have a lot of intelligence *and* a strong Intellect. The combination of a lot of intelligence with a strong Intellect sets them apart from other people.

You can see that the Intellect is related to these other terms, but it is not the same as any of them. It specifically refers to the human power to think, reason, compare, posit, infer, judge and decide. So, what exactly does the Intellect *do*? And how does it set us apart from other forms of life? Let's explore that question now and discover the extraordinary gift that makes us uniquely human.

You have probably noticed that there are often a lot of thoughts and feelings in your Mind that seem to flow freely, without any particular order. This is just part of what it is to be human! But while it might feel a little chaotic sometimes, when you compare it to plants and animals, you will see that it's actually far more advanced, intricate, and special.

Let's look at the differences between plants, animals, and humans to see just what makes us unique:

- Plants only have physical body. There is nothing inside them that directs them to act. They grow, reproduce, and die—that is all.

- Animals have a Mind in addition to their physical body. Their Mind allows them to move around and act on their instinctive desires, but they do so without thinking.

- Only humans have a body, Mind, *and* Intellect— the unique power to think, reason, and decide.

So it is specifically the Intellect that makes us special among all living things. We alone have the power to focus on a single thought out of the flowing river of thoughts in the Mind. This gift carries with it both great potential and great responsibility — the ability to shape not only our own lives but to understand our connection to all other beings.

To be even more specific, it is the dance between the Intellect and the Mind that makes us unique. If we don't use our Intellect well, we're not much different from animals. This is because we are not taking advantage of the one feature that sets us apart — the feature that allows us to contemplate our place in the Infinity of existence.

What does it mean to use the Intellect well?

- **First, we have to recognize the Intellect as a separate power within us.** It's not enough to take for granted that we are able to "think," and leave it at that. When we "think," what we are actually doing is applying our Intellect to the flowing thoughts in our Mind. The Mind and the Intellect are two separate parts of us working together in a beautiful harmony.

- **Then, we have to use the Intellect to Concentrate.** *Concentration is the capacity of the Intellect to guide the Mind to continue its present activity, without allowing the Mind to slip into past experiences or future expectations, with a view to accomplishing a clear Goal.* Concentration is the key to using the Intellect well — and to understanding the deeper truths

11

about ourselves, our relationships, and our universe.

Before applying your Intellect, the thoughts that exist in your Mind are no more than **desires and emotions**. They are uncontrolled wants that naturally arise just from being alive. It can be frustrating to have a lot of desires that we can't fulfill, and without the help of the Intellect, our desires can actually make us *unhappy*! This is one of the greatest paradoxes of human existence—that the very thoughts that can lead us to fulfillment can also lead us astray.

But when you concentrate and apply your Intellect on one desire, that desire then becomes something else—a **goal**. Once a desire becomes a goal, you can reflect on it and pursue it in a more meaningful way. Why should we care about this? Because achieving goals can make us happy! In fact, this transformation—from chaotic desires to focused goals—is one of the most wonderful processes we can experience as human beings.

Here's how it works:

- Let's say you have a certain number of unfulfilled desires in your Mind. You're used or conditioned to these existing desires remaining unfulfilled, and even though they are unfulfilled, you are at ease with them.

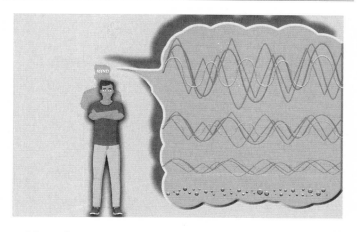

- Now let's say a new desire is added. This new unfulfilled desire disturbs the peace of your Mind, making you feel agitated.

- Thankfully, you have a strong Intellect. You are able to use your Intellect to focus on this new desire and turn it into a goal. By continuing to concentrate, you eventually fulfill this goal.

A sense of happiness comes over you as you release this unfulfilled desire.

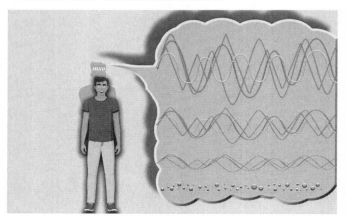

When you achieve goals, you become happy by reducing your agitation. And the only way to achieve goals is to use your Intellect! This is why it is so important to know that your Intellect and your Mind are separate, and that they must work together in harmony to bring you happiness. This harmony is not just beautiful in itself—it's a mirror of the greater harmony that exists throughout the universe.

Remember the specific difference between them:

- Your **Intellect** is the power within you that allows you to think, reason, and make decisions.

- Your **Mind** is a collection of unfulfilled desires, emotions. New desires constantly appear here, and it is up to the Intellect to fulfill them.

These two qualities are part of something even more remarkable called **the inner personality**. The inner personality is the essence within each of us that uses thoughts to guide our lives. Each part of the inner personality has a different role and interacts with thoughts in specific ways. Together, they form an intricate symphony that makes each of us who we are.

Apart from the Mind and the Intellect, there are two other parts of the inner personality. Just to make you aware of them, we will briefly introduce them here. They will be explored in more detail later, as we continue to unfold the magnificent complexity of human Consciousness.

- **The memory** is the part of the inner personality that holds all of your past experiences in the form of thoughts.

- **The ego** is the part of the inner personality that recognizes your entire self as one being, and declares that being to be your identity.

These two parts, along with the Mind and Intellect, form the inner personality. Each of them plays a separate, specific role in what makes you uniquely you. Just as every star in the night sky has its own special place in the cosmos, each of these components has its own vital role to play. Again, the role that each of these parts plays will be described in more detail throughout this book.

You may encounter some people who feel it is unnecessary to understand these separate parts, or who deny their importance. They may feel that thought is thought, and that's all they need to know. To such people, Mind, Intellect, memory, and ego are all the same, and there's nothing to be gained by studying them further.

A person like this might be lucky enough to have just a sufficient level of Intellect, which will allow them to have a reasonably okay life. But there will always be a limit to how strong their Intellect can be—and to how happy and fulfilled a life they will lead! This is because they lack an understanding of the beautiful relationship between the Intellect, the

Mind, and the other parts that make up who we are. It's like having a map to a vast treasure, but never learning how to read it.

In order to live a happy and fulfilled life, it is vital that you recognize the role of the Intellect and understand how to use it. All the ideas we will explore in this book are connected to the wonder of the Intellect and depend on your ability to use the Intellect well. Through understanding and strengthening your Intellect, you begin a remarkable journey—one that can lead not only to personal fulfillment but to a deeper connection with the universe itself.

When you think of personal fulfillment, what thoughts arise in your Mind? In the next chapter, we'll explore the idea of fulfillment by looking at the different kinds of goals that humans may set. In doing so, we will discover how these goals can contribute not only to your happiness but to your understanding of your place in the vast tapestry of existence.

Chapter 02

Human Goals

———— ❧❧ ————

Despite our differences from plants and animals, there are a number of things we share with them. These are our fundamental needs: to eat, rest, reproduce, and protect ourselves from danger. When it comes to these four basic needs, humans are just like any other living thing on Earth—all of us bound together by these common necessities of life.

The one thing that sets us apart from other forms of life is the way we go about satisfying our needs. Because humans can create goals, we are able to plan for the future. This means we can take deliberate actions that help us meet our needs. This extraordinary ability to transform our needs into goals is one of the most beautiful aspects of being human.

As we saw in the last chapter, **the Intellect is what allows us to set goals**. This is why it is so important to use the Intellect well. Not only will it help you meet your basic needs, but it can also help you to live a happy and fulfilled life—and perhaps even understand deeper truths about your place in the universe.

In the previous chapter, we also pointed out how our desires flow freely in our Minds before they are turned into goals. Even so, when desires are turned into goals, they always fall into one of three basic categories. Let's explore each of these categories now and see how they relate to your journey through life.

The first category includes goals of security and survival. These goals have to do with meeting the basic needs of life. There are four types of basic needs:

- Food
- Clothing
- Shelter
- Health

Different people may have different requirements. For example, a wealthier person may require more food and finer clothing to consider their needs met, while a less well-off person may be satisfied with only basic food and clothing.

Even so, these goals of security are the basic needs of all people, connecting us in our shared human experience.

When we form deep bonds with others—whether family, friends, or partners—we often find these basic needs easier to meet. Not only can supportive relationships provide practical assistance, but the emotional security of truly understanding and being understood by another person helps bring peace to our Minds, making us better equipped to face life's challenges. This reflects one of the most beautiful aspects of human connection: our ability to help each other feel secure, both physically and emotionally.

The second category includes goals of comfort, luxury, and entertainment. These goals have to do with satisfying the desires humans crave beyond the basic necessities of life. These goals may include things like:

- Extra comfort, like traveling in first class
- Luxurious possessions, like jewelry or fancy cars
- Recreation, such as trips to faraway places

These goals of comfort can only be pursued once the goals of security are mostly or completely achieved. This means that they are usually only available to people who enjoy more well-off positions in society. Yet even these goals of comfort point to something deeper—a human yearning that extends beyond mere survival. And when shared with those we deeply care about, these comforts take on new meaning; a journey becomes more than just travel when experienced with someone who helps us see the world through fresh eyes.

Thus, even though these additional comforts exceed what is strictly necessary for survival, they can genuinely lead to happiness and fulfillment— especially when shared with the people you love.

The third category includes goals of invisible wealth. What does this mean? Invisible wealth is what contributes to unexpected positive events in your life. This may include things like being born into a good family or winning the lottery. You do nothing to cause these events, and yet they happen anyway.

Now, you may be wondering, if you cannot control these events, how can this be a goal? The answer is that you cannot control them in *this* life. But your invisible wealth in this life is the result of actions taken in previous lives. This means that in this life you can set goals that will contribute to your invisible wealth in future lives.

The depth of your relationships and how you treat those close to you can play an important role here, though we'll explore this fascinating connection more fully in later chapters when we talk more about past and future lives. For now, here is a brief description of what this means in the context of invisible wealth:

- When a person dies, their physical body is broken down and returns to the Earth. In this way, their body is not really gone. Instead, it is preserved and transformed.

- In the same way, the thoughts that exist in your inner personality are not destroyed at death. They are preserved and transformed, and will come back as a new inner personality in another life.

- This means that the effects of the goals you set and achieve in one life carry over to the next life.

By committing good deeds in one life, you can accumulate invisible wealth for future lives. So, while goals of security and comfort both have outcomes in *this* life, goals of invisible wealth will have outcomes in the *next* life. In this way, your actions reach far beyond your immediate existence, touching lives you may never know.

These are the three main categories of human goals: security, comfort, and invisible wealth.

Unfortunately, life is not as simple as just setting goals, achieving them, and becoming happy. Why not? It's because **each of these goals has built-in flaws that bring some amount of unhappiness**.

- **The first flaw is the pain and suffering that is involved in pursuing your goals**. Even if it makes you happy to achieve a goal, there is some amount of unhappiness involved in the pain and suffering that comes with pursuing it. Simply put, achieving goals requires work, and work is not always pleasant!

- **The second flaw is the dissatisfaction you feel when you achieve your goals**. When you achieve a goal, you become happy—but there is always some other unfulfilled goal you could still achieve that would make you *even happier*. So you will feel some amount of dissatisfaction, because you could always feel just a little bit happier than you are right now.

- **The third flaw is the sense of attachment you feel when you achieve your goals**. Imagine that you had a crush on someone, and you set a goal of winning their affection. Then, imagine that you succeed in your goal and you start dating that person. You will certainly feel some happiness from achieving your goal! But you will also start to experience new fears, too—like the fear of losing that person from your life. This fear comes from becoming attached to your partner as a source of happiness. This is why attachment is another major cause of unhappiness that goes along with achieving your goals.

Later in this book, we will explore ways to live that can help reduce the unhappiness you may feel when you achieve your goals. These approaches will help you live a happier and more fulfilled life, in harmony with the true nature of existence.

In addition to these three main categories of goal, there is also a rare fourth type of goal. **This fourth goal is known through various terminologies namely Liberation or Salvation or Self-Realization or Capturing Infinity**—a state of Infinite happiness that enters you when you become one with the deepest secrets of existence. While it's worth knowing that this goal exists, it's really not necessary to be concerned with it now.

It is very rare for humans to even set, let alone achieve this goal. As we have seen, unfulfilled goals can cause agitation and unhappiness. Because it is so rare to achieve this goal, it is more likely to cause unhappiness than happiness. So, while we will mention this goal from time to time in this book, it's better not to worry about it. Just know that it exists, but focus on the other three categories of goals, which are much more likely to increase your sense of happiness and fulfillment in this life.

Now, let us briefly return to the Intellect. We know that the Intellect is responsible for helping us set goals. **In order to use the Intellect well, we need to understand how it fits in with all the other aspects of who we are.** In the next chapter, we will explore the incredible complexity of human nature, helping you get a better idea of how the Intellect fits into the bigger picture of what makes you uniquely *you*.

Chapter 03

Non-Anatomical Composition

————— ✿✿ —————

We have already seen how important it is to recognize the relationship between the Intellect and the Mind. Just understanding this beautiful interplay will help you set goals and live a better life.

Your ability to do these things will deepen even further if you understand how the Intellect fits in with all the other parts of what makes you who you are. With that in mind, this chapter will explore the entire human composition in detail, revealing the intricate harmony of elements that make human existence possible.

Humans are made up of eleven main factors, each of which falls into one of three categories. These categories are:

- **Bodies.** Every human contains three bodies.

- **Personality layers.** Every human contains five personality layers.

- **States of experience.** Every human alternates between three states of experience.

By the end of this chapter, we will have explored each of these categories and factors in depth. Let's begin now with the first category — the bodies.

The Bodies

Every person (including you!) has three different types of body. They are: **the gross body**, which is the physical body; **the subtle body**, which contains the inner personality, along with a few other components; and **the causal body**, a new concept that we will discover soon.

As we explore these bodies, we will use the same method to explore each one.

- First, we will look at the body's **raw materials** — the basic building blocks that make it up.

- Second, we will look at the body's **components**. These are the larger structures that exist within each body.

- Third, we will look at the **functions** of each body. Functions are the actions that the body carries out.

- Fourth, we will look at the **nature** of each body. The nature of a body refers to what it is "like" — the unique characteristics that make it what it is.

Now, let's begin with the gross body – the most visible aspect of our existence.

Gross Body

While the term *gross* often means "disgusting" or "offensive," it has a very different meaning here. Instead of referring to something undesirable, in this context, it simply means "tangible" or "physically apparent." The significance of this will become clear in a moment.

The raw material of the gross body is gross matter. Gross matter refers to anything that you can see and touch—the tangible, physical things that make up our world.

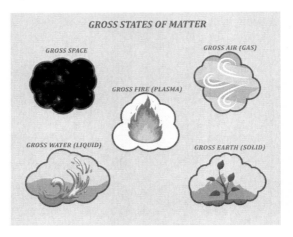

GROSS STATES OF MATTER

GROSS SPACE

GROSS AIR (GAS)

GROSS FIRE (PLASMA)

GROSS WATER (LIQUID)

GROSS EARTH (SOLID)

The gross body is made up of a combination of the five fundamental states of gross matter, which are:

- The gaseous state, which is also known as air

- The liquid state, which is also known as water

- The solid state, which is also known as earth

- The plasma state, which is also known as fire

- The 'Space', the fifth fundamental state of matter, proven by science

These five states combine in countless ways to create every aspect of our physical form, much like how the various aspects of our relationships—thoughts, feelings, and actions—combine to create something greater than their individual parts. Their combinations make up all the **components** of the physical body. While the gross body contains many components, there are three major categories of them:

- **Organs of perception**. These are the eyes (sight), ears (hearing), skin (touch), tongue (taste), and nose (smell)

- **Organs of action**. These are the mouth (speech), hands (manipulation), legs (locomotion), excretory organs (excretion), and reproductive organs (reproduction)

- **Involuntary organs**. These are the organs that sustain life without our involvement, such as the lungs, heart, digestive tract, and so on

These components allow the gross body to carry out its function. Simply put, **the function of the gross body is to allow us to exert actions and experience their consequences**.

Now, what about its nature? There are four aspects of the nature of the gross body, each reflecting a profound truth about our physical existence:

- **Cyclical change**. The body goes through a cycle of changes, starting with birth, progressing through maturity to old age, and then death. After death, the body's gross matter returns to the Earth, giving way to new life. So, the changes are cyclical.

- **Continuous change**. The changes in that cycle flow smoothly and continuously from one to the next. The gross body is always changing, always in motion.

- **Finite lifespan**. The average human lifespan is around seventy-two years. Some will live longer, others shorter, but all have a finite lifespan.

- **Tangibility and perceptibility**. Because it is made of gross matter, the gross body is perceptible to both oneself and to others.

So much for the gross body. Let's now consider something more mysterious—the subtle body.

Subtle Body

You're probably wondering what the word *subtle* is supposed to mean here. Before we get into this section, let's explore that question.

Subtlety refers to the relationship between two different things. **One thing is subtler than another when it both controls *and* pervades within it and beyond**. Just as deeper understanding in a relationship comes from looking beneath surface interactions, the subtle body operates on a deeper level than the gross body.

We have already pointed out how the inner personality is responsible for controlling our actions. To be more precise, the entire subtle body is responsible for controlling the entire gross body. (Something is *gross* when it is less *subtle* than something else.) This relationship is why the subtle body and gross body have those particular names.

You will see the words *gross* and *subtle* used to describe different things throughout this book. When you do, remember what they refer to: one thing *controlling* and *pervading within* and beyond another thing.

With that said, we are ready to begin our exploration of the subtle body, starting with its raw materials.

Just as the gross body is made of gross matter, **the subtle body is made of subtle matter**. This is its raw material. And what is subtle matter? **It is composed of combinations of pure states of matter**. This idea is a little tricky to grasp, but here's how it works:

• No state of gross matter can ever really be pure, because it always contains some amount of the other states of gross matter. Even the "purest" water will contain trapped air and trace minerals, have some temperature, and occupy space.

- **Pure states of matter, then, can only exist in the form of thoughts**. Only in thoughts can all other states of matter be excluded, leaving only a single, pure state.

- In the form of thoughts, pure states of matter can combine and yet still remain pure. These combinations are known as subtle matter, and are what our complex thoughts are made of.

Therefore, All the Love you have right now, in the present (life), All the Love you had in the past (lives), and All the Love you will have in your future (lives) - all tantamount to pure Matter! YOUR THOUGHTS ARE MADE OF MATTER!

In short, combinations of pure states of matter make up subtle matter, and subtle matter makes up thoughts. So when we refer to subtle matter as the raw material of the subtle body, this is what we are referring to.

Let's move on to talk about the various *components* of the subtle body. There are twenty of them, evenly spread across four separate categories. Because there are so many, we will mention the functions of these components as we introduce them. We will also go more quickly through the first three categories and spend a little more time with the final one.

The first three categories of the subtle body are as follows:

- **The five power centers of perception** give us the power to register sensory information from the outside world. **The subtle eye** gives us the power of sight; **the subtle ear**, the power of hearing; **the subtle skin**, the power of touch; **the subtle tongue**, the power of taste; and **the subtle nose**, the power of smell.

  - Note the relationship between these components and their gross counterparts. The gross eye sees; the subtle eye *enables* the power of sight.

  - The function of these components is to act as an intermediary between the gross organs of perception and the Mind, where our thoughts collect.

- **The five power centers of action** give us the power to manifest our decisions as actions in the world. These are the power centers of **speech**, **manipulation**, **locomotion**, **excretion**, and **reproduction**.

  - Again, these power centers do not actually *perform* these actions; instead, they allow the corresponding gross organs to perform them.

  - The function of these components is to act as an intermediary between the Mind, where the Intellect makes decisions, and the gross organs that carry out the relevant actions.

- **The five power centers of bodily function** give us the power to automatically sustain healthy life. These are the power centers of **breathing, digesting, blood circulation, waste filtering,** and **reversal** (e.g. vomiting, sneezing, tearing up, etc.).

  - The function of these components is to ensure that the entire gross body remains healthy so that the subtle body may continue to function.

The final five components make up what we have already referred to as **the inner personality**. We already named four of them: **the Mind, the Intellect, the memory,** and **the ego**. What about the fifth component? The truth is, the Intellect actually consists of two parts—a gross Intellect and a subtle Intellect.

The subtle Intellect is involved in matters relating to merging with the universe. The gross Intellect is involved in everything else. Because this book is primarily concerned with helping you live a happy and fulfilled life, we will continue to refer to *the Intellect* as such, even though we specifically mean *the gross Intellect*.

Though we have already briefly touched on the functions of these components, let's explore them more deeply now because they are important to understand:

- **The Mind** is where our flowing thoughts gather—both the everyday thoughts that help us navigate the world and the deeper feelings that arise from our connections with others. It's the place where we first experience the joy of friendship, the warmth of love, and yes, sometimes the challenge of difficult emotions too. The Intellect exercises its power here, helping us understand and work with these thoughts and feelings. Think of the Mind as a garden where many different plants grow— some that we cultivated intentionally, others that sprouted on their own. Every garden needs both natural growth and careful tending. **The Mind's function is to serve as a bridge between the fifteen power centers and the decisive action of the Intellect, creating a harmonious partnership that allows us to grow and thrive.**

- **The Intellect** is not just a cold, analytical force— it's the power that helps us understand our thoughts and feelings deeply enough to act on them wisely. When we feel strong emotions about someone we care for, the Intellect helps us respond in ways that nurture the relationship rather than harm it. **Its function is to work with the Mind to turn thoughts into decisive actions that serve our growth and deepen our connections.**

- **The memory** is the place where all of our experiences are recorded and stored. All perceptions, all actions, all thoughts and feelings—everything, from this life and past ones, is stored here. **Its function is to shape our gross and subtle bodies, both when we are first born and continuing throughout life**.

- **The ego** is a specific train of thought that recognizes one's current gross and subtle body as oneself. This is a simple, factual declaration of the relationship between those two things. **The function of the ego is to provide a constant point of reference as a person goes through life; it helps us keep track of who we are**.

Now, as to the nature of the subtle body, there are three main aspects, each revealing something profound about our inner existence:

- **Constant change.** Just as relationships grow and evolve over time, new thoughts and desires constantly arise in the Mind and shape the character of our subtle bodies. If the Intellect is strong and works in harmony with the Mind, together they can direct these thoughts toward positive action; if this partnership is weak, we may act according to momentary whims. In either case, change is constant in the subtle body.

- **Finite lifespan**. Like the gross body, the subtle body has a finite lifespan. But it is much longer. When a gross body dies, the subtle body returns in a new gross body. But when the universe ends, either in a Big Rip or Big Crunch, the subtle body also comes to an end. So the lifespan of the subtle body is the lifespan of the universe. (We will discuss the universe in more detail in the chapter on Creation.)

- **Perceptibility**. Recall that the nature of the gross body is that it is perceptible to both ourselves and to others. The subtle body is also perceptible — to an extent. Each person's subtle body is perceptible only to themselves. It is not perceptible to other people. This is the third nature of the subtle body.

With that, our exploration of the subtle body is complete, and we are ready to discover something even more elusive and awe-inspiring – the causal body.

Causal Body

In order to understand the causal body, we first need to briefly discuss what causality means in the first place. In general, causality refers to the relationship between cause and effect. You smile at someone, and they smile back; you knock over a glass of water, and it falls from the table and spills on the floor.

In the context of this book, **causality specifically refers to the state that exists before *and after* the existence of the universe.**

The universe as we know it is full of gross and subtle matter. It came into being during the Big Bang, and one day, far in the future, it will come to an end during a Big Crunch or Big Rip. But it is important to note that this "end" doesn't mean that everything in the universe will be destroyed. It will simply be transformed into another state, until, at some point down the line, it is transformed again and gives way to a new Big Bang and a new universe.

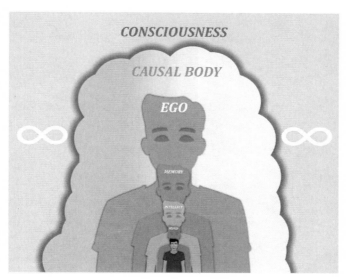

The period between the end of one universe and the beginning of the next can be referred to as the **causal universe**. The causal universe contains all the potential for the next universe, in much the same way that a seed contains the potential for a tree. Once the tree begins to grow, the seed ceases to exist; it has released its potential into the tree.

In this way, we can understand that the causal body contains the potential for our gross body and the subtle body in this universe. Because it contains these things in their potential form only, rather than a form with actual attributes, our four-part exploration of it will be brief.

- **The raw material of the causal body is causal matter**. Causal matter is nothing but the potential for gross and subtle matter.

- **There are only two components of the causal body**: the seed forms of the gross and subtle bodies.

- **The function of the causal body is to serve as a resting place for the gross and subtle bodies in the period between universes.**

- **The nature** of the causal body is threefold:

  - **Cyclical change**. The causal body is a link in the chain of creation and destruction of the other two bodies.

- **Infinite lifespan**. While the gross and subtle bodies are periodically destroyed, the causal body is eternal. There is no end to its lifespan—only periodic interruption.

- **Imperceptibility**. Unlike the other two bodies, the causal body is completely imperceptible, even to oneself.

These three bodies make up the first three factors of the human composition: the gross body, which takes in sensory information and performs actions; the subtle body, which receives external information and decides what to do about it; and the causal body, which holds the potential for the other two bodies in the interval between universes.

Let's now move on to explore the other factors of the human composition, beginning with the personality layers.

The Personality Layers

The next factors in the human composition are the five personality layers. **These layers are responsible for creating the power for the bodies to do what they do**; they allow the components of the three bodies to perform their functions and fulfill their natures. One layer corresponds to the gross body, three correspond to the subtle body, and one corresponds to the causal body, totaling five layers.

- **The Food Layer:** The personality layer that corresponds to the gross body is known as **the food layer**. This layer contains the body's power to grow and decay. It gets its name from the fact that the cycle of growth and decay is driven by food.

What does that mean? It means that even before you were born, food that your parents consumed turned into the biological material that would later create you. Then, once you were born, all the growth that you have experienced in life has come from the food you have eaten. And one day, when you die, your gross body will become food for microbes. They will turn your body back into raw organic material that will eventually create more food, and the cycle will begin again. The food layer of the personality contains the power for the gross body to grow and decay in this way.

Now let's talk about the three layers that are connected with the subtle body. They are:

- **The vital energy layer**: This layer corresponds to the five power centers of action and the five power centers of bodily function. It contains the power for the body to break down the food it takes in, turn it into energy, and use that energy for actions. This energy also powers the activity of the next two layers. You can think of it as a bridge between the gross body and the next two layers namely the mental layer and the Intellectual layer.

- **The mental layer**: This layer corresponds to the five power centers of perception, along with the Mind, memory, and ego. It contains the power to take in information, generate new desires, and command the vital energy layer to perform actions.

  - New desires are constantly being generated here. This is because new information constantly flows into the mental layer. Information about the outside world flows in through the power centers of perception, while internal information also flows in from the memory and ego.

43

- It is important to note that **the Mind constantly directs the vital energy layer to perform actions**. This happens whether or not the Intellect is involved in turning actions into goals. The power of the mental layer causes the Mind to direct the vital energy layer to act.

- **The Intellectual layer**: This layer corresponds to the five power centers of perception, along with the Intellect, memory, and ego. It contains the power of knowing, which means examining information, deciding what to do about it, and directing the Mind how to behave.

  - This layer helps you to set goals and increase your happiness in two ways. First, it allows you to set and achieve goals, which can make you happier. Second, it allows you to dismiss unnecessary desires, which helps you avoid unhappiness.

  - How can it be that several of these components also belong to the mental layer? It's because both the Intellect *and* the Mind engage with thoughts and desires. With a weaker Intellect, thoughts flow indiscriminately in the Mind; with a stronger Intellect, the thought flows in the Mind are controlled and regulated.

To put the three layers of the subtle body into perspective, the Intellectual layer *knows*, the mental layer *desires*, and the vital energy layer *acts* in order to fulfill those desires.

The Bliss Layer: The fifth layer of the personality is known as **the bliss layer**, and it is associated with the causal body. This layer has the power to suppress the activity of the other four layers. This is the power that asserts itself during the period between universes, when the causal body contains the potential for the gross and subtle bodies. In this life, it is also associated with the state of deep sleep—one of the three states of experience, which we will now explore.

The States of Experience

The final three factors of the human composition are the three states of experience. They are: **the waking state**, **the dream state**, and **the deep sleep state**. Throughout your whole life, you will always be in one of these three states.

As we explore these states, we will use this method to explore each one:

- First, we will look at **the state of the subtle body**—what is the condition of the Mind, Intellect, memory, and ego during this state?

- Second, we will look at **the nature of the state**— what is the experience "like"?

- Third, we will look at **the predominant medium of each state**—which aspect of the body is most predominant during this state?

Now, let's begin with the first state: the waking state.

- During the waking state, **the subtle body is fully functional**. It is fully available to gather new experiences, generate new desires, obtain new knowledge, and direct the body to perform new action.

- **The nature of the waking state is external, physical, and objective**. This means that, while you are awake, you are constantly experiencing physical objects and sensations in the world around you.

- **The predominant medium of the waking state is the gross body**. This is because, during the waking state, we are constantly experiencing physical things and taking physical actions. These things depend on the gross body, which is why we say that it is the predominant medium.

Now for the second state of experience—the dream state.

- During the dream state, **the memory is the only part of the subtle body that is active**. And what is it doing? Consider this. During the waking state, new thoughts are constantly generated.

The Intellect tries to examine them all, but there are always too many. Unexamined thoughts get temporarily stored in the memory. **During the dream state, these unexamined thoughts are thrown out as random images**. This is the only activity the subtle body performs in this state.

- **The nature of the dream state is internal and subjective**. This means that, unlike the waking state, which involves interaction with the wider world, the experience of the dream state is limited to your own inner self.

- **The predominant medium of the dream state is the subtle body—specifically the memory**. The entire experience of the dream state is centered on the memory, which is why we can say that the memory predominates.

Then there is the deep sleep state, the third state of experience and the final factor of the human composition.

- In the deep sleep state, **the subtle body is entirely non-functional**. Remember that we said this state of experience corresponds to the bliss layer of the human personality. In this state, all other powers of the body are suppressed. In fact, you can't even "experience" this state of experience while you are in deep sleep; you can only notice and register that it has occurred after you have woken up.

47

- **The nature of the deep sleep state is total ignorance**. Because your other powers are suppressed, they are unavailable to you in this state. This means that you cannot experience anything, consider anything, or take any action during this state.

- **The predominant medium of the deep sleep state is the causal body**. We can say this because we can observe that neither the gross nor the subtle body is active at all during this state. The activity of those bodies exists in a state of potential—which is the definition of the causal body.

With that, our exploration of the eleven factors of the human composition is complete. While this may seem like a lot of information, understanding these aspects of yourself is vital to living your life well. This knowledge will add to your intelligence and will help you strengthen both your Intellect and its harmonious partnership with your Mind. Both of these things are necessary if you want to be able to set goals well and live a fulfilled life!

Now that we have completed this full inventory of what makes you who you are, we will move on to explore an even deeper mystery—the nature of Consciousness itself.

Chapter 04

Consciousness and You

———❊❊———

Previously, we mentioned that the Gross Body, Subtle Body, and the Causal Body are made of the five fundamental states of matter. Matter is something naturally inert and insentient. But if that is the case, then how is it that we are able to be conscious and able to think? It implies that we must have borrowed Consciousness from another independent original source of Consciousness, and that source of Consciousness must be non-material in nature!

What *is* Consciousness, and where does it come from? Just as two people in love might feel they share one heart while remaining separate beings, Consciousness exists both as an Infinite whole and as individual reflections within us. Understanding this paradox is key to understanding not just

Consciousness itself, but the profound connection that exists between all beings.

Scientists suggest that Consciousness is created by the brain, which is made of gross matter. Based on the definition of *subtlety* that we explored earlier, though, we know that Consciousness is subtler than the brain. So how can Consciousness originate there? It's not possible.

Others, like psychologists and philosophers, suggest that Consciousness originates in the Mind. We know that this is wrong because, for one thing, they don't even have an accurate understanding of the entire subtle body. Beyond that, we know that the subtle body is also made of matter, meaning that it is impossible for Consciousness to originate there.

So where *does* Consciousness come from? If we know that all matter is inert, then we have to conclude that it must have a source that has nothing to do with gross, subtle, or causal matter. **This source is something called *pure Consciousness*, and it exists totally separate from all types of matter**.

This means that you don't actually "possess" Consciousness, but only "borrow" it, in much the same way that the moon borrows its silvery light from the sun. Think about moonlight for a moment—the moon appears to shine with its own radiance, yet it's actually reflecting the sun's light.

Similarly, when we feel conscious and aware, we're actually reflecting a universal Consciousness that illuminates all existence. You can think of yourself as being bathed in Consciousness, like a flower opening its petals to the morning light.

This borrowed nature of Consciousness tells us something profound about how we relate to each other and to the world. Just as the moon and planets all reflect the same sunlight while appearing to shine independently, every conscious being reflects the same pure Consciousness while appearing to have their own separate awareness. When you feel deeply connected to another person—whether a romantic partner, close friend, or family member—you're catching a glimpse of this shared Consciousness that exists within all beings.

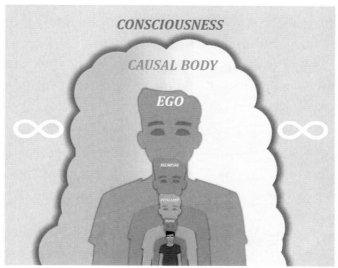

Consciousness makes us aware of ourselves. But what is the Self, anyway? Consider this profound question:

- **Anything that belongs to you is not you**. You wouldn't say that your cell phone *is* you—it only belongs to you. Similarly, no other material thing, including your gross and subtle body, *is* you either. This shows that "you" are something other than your material bodies.

- **Anything that you experience is not you**. An experience happens when a subject— "I"— interacts with some other object. Because all your bodies are made of matter, they can all be considered as objects. So we know that "I" must be something other than those bodies.

This tells us something important about the self. It tells us that the Self exists separately from our three material bodies, so it must be some fourth "thing" that is not like the others—something more subtle and mysterious than anything we can see or touch.

When you truly connect with another person, you might feel that the boundary between you seems to fade away. This isn't just poetic language— it's pointing toward a deeper truth about existence. The Consciousness that knows "I am" in you is the same Consciousness that knows "I am" in them. The only difference is that it's being reflected through different subtle bodies, like the same light being reflected by different mirrors.

So far, we have defined Consciousness and the self using negatives. How can we describe these things positively? Consider the following indicators of Consciousness to get a better idea of what this extraordinary force really is:

- **Consciousness is non-material**. Because the nature of all matter is that it is inert, we know that Consciousness must be something other than matter.

- **Consciousness is independent**. Because matter is inert, it cannot generate anything subtler than itself. So we know that Consciousness cannot be generated by the material universe, which means that it is independent from it.

- **Consciousness does not have attributes**. Only material objects have attributes. Because Consciousness is non-material, it cannot have attributes. (This is why we used the word "indicators" a moment ago—the things on this list only *indicate* what Consciousness is, because it doesn't actually have attributes.)

- **Consciousness is eternal**. The material universe is bound by the four dimensions—one of which is time. Because Consciousness is independent of the material universe, it is also independent of time.

- **Consciousness transcends space**. For the same reason as above, Consciousness is independent of space.

- **Consciousness is All-Pervading, exists all throughout space and beyond**. This may seem to contradict the previous statement, but it does not. While two material things cannot occupy the same space at the same time, Consciousness does not have that same limitation. This means that it exists everywhere, all throughout space and beyond, hence All-Pervading.

- **Consciousness is real**. What do we mean by real? *Real* essentially means "permanent". Anything that is temporary is not really real. But because Consciousness is permanent, it is the only thing that is real.

- **Consciousness is the Knowing principle**. The only thing that separates you, a self-aware entity, from inert objects, which lack awareness, is Consciousness. So we can see that Consciousness is what gives us the power of knowledge and awareness.

- **Consciousness is happiness**. Think back to the chapter on goals. We talked about how eliminating unfulfilled desires makes you happy. Because desires are thoughts, and thoughts are made of subtle matter, we know that happiness cannot be generated from inert matter, the thoughts themselves. So we can conclude that happiness you experience is actually part of Consciousness, and that as we eliminate unfulfilled desires, we are eliminating obstacles to our experience of happiness.

All this leaves one question unanswered. If Consciousness is everywhere, why doesn't it enliven all inert matter the same way it has enlivened humans and other living beings? The answer has to do with the subtle body. **The subtle body is the instrument that allows inert matter to become conscious**. Only beings that have a subtle body can exhibit Consciousness, even though Consciousness flows through inert objects like metal and stone just the same as it flows through us.

Think of it like this: When you meet someone new, you might sense their basic humanity but not feel particularly connected. As you get to know them better, your subtle bodies—your thoughts, feelings, and understanding—begin to resonate. The more deeply you understand each other, the more you recognize yourself in them. This mirrors how Consciousness itself works: While it exists everywhere, it can only be reflected where there's a subtle body to receive it.

This understanding of Consciousness reveals something remarkable about our existence. **While we often think of ourselves as separate from the world around us, we are actually participating in the same flow of Consciousness that permeates all of existence.**

This means that the same eternal Consciousness that flows through you is *also* flowing through every other person in your life! So even though you have your own body and your own set of experiences, you are actually intimately connected with all people on a level that almost transcends understanding. This is the true meaning of the title of this book—*The You in Me, Forever.*

This astonishing connection goes even further; it applies to *physical* things as well! The only difference between humans and inert things is that our subtle bodies allow us to become aware of this Consciousness, while a stone or piece of metal, lacking a subtle body, remains unaware.

This description should give you a deeper understanding of what Consciousness is. This understanding will be important when we discuss the ways to live that can help you set goals, eliminate desires, and lead a fulfilling life. We are almost ready to begin that part of the conversation—but first, let's take a closer look at our place in creation so that we can have a deeper understanding of how we fit into the Infinite expanse of the cosmos.

Chapter 05

Creation, Big Bang(s)

———— ❦ ————

Before we begin exploring ways to live a more fulfilled life, there's one final piece of understanding we need to put in place—our position in the Infinite web of the universe. Once we understand where we came from and where we're going, we'll be able to grasp the cycles that define human existence—and see how deeply interconnected we truly are, not just in Consciousness but in our very physical nature.

*Note: The context of the subject necessitates discussing Creation / Big Bang, but only bare minimum details are discussed in this book. A much more detailed discussion on Creation & Big Bang can be found in the book **"Who Banged the Big Bang!"** written by the same Author.*

While science tells us that the universe began with the Big Bang billions of years ago and will eventually end in either a Big Rip or Big Crunch, this doesn't begin to reveal the profound mystery of how our universe actually came to be—or how its creation reflects the deep unity that exists between all things.

Let's start with what existed before the universe as we know it. We've already talked about causal matter, and how our causal bodies contain the potential that will eventually become our gross and subtle bodies. **The entire collection of causal matter that contains the potential for every gross**

and subtle thing in our universe is known as the *causal universe.* Just as the potential for every human relationship exists before two people meet, this causal universe contains the potential for everything that would eventually manifest in our world.

But the causal universe isn't the only thing that existed at that point. In the last chapter, we talked about how Consciousness is eternal — existing everywhere, in everything, always. So Consciousness existed at that point too — and **it was Consciousness in combination with the resultants of all past actions of all subtle bodies of the previous universe that gave the causal universe**

the push it needed to release its potential and give way to our current universe.

What happened next reveals something extraordinary about the nature of creation. All of that potential was manifested in order from the most to the least subtle, resulting in the universe we have today. But this did not happen in a single event, as the current Big Bang theory suggests. **Instead, it happened in two phases — a Subtle Big Bang and a Gross Big Bang**. Understanding these events helps us see how deeply connected we all are, both in our inner nature and our physical form.

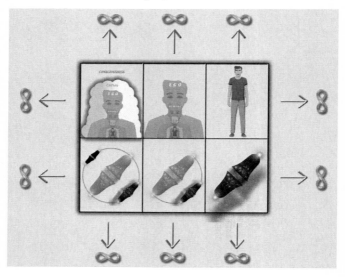

The first thing that occurs during the Subtle Big Bang is the formation of all subtle matter. You will remember that subtle matter consists of the five pure states of fundamental matter. These are created in a specific order. Note that each of these states is also associated with a specific sensory property. The order of their creation, along with their related sensory properties, is as follows:

- Space – sound
- Air (gas) – touch
- Fire (plasma) – sight
- Water (liquid) – taste
- Earth (solid) – smell

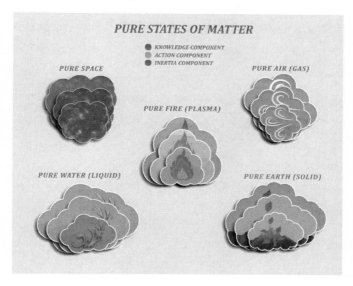

In addition to these sensory properties, each pure state of matter also contains three intrinsic properties, akin to what we observe in the functioning of the observed gross universe:

- Knowledge

- Action

- Inertia

These intrinsic properties guide the way both the Subtle and Gross Big Bangs unfold, creating the foundations for all future connections and relationships in the universe.

First, the intrinsic knowledge property asserts itself. This leads to the formation of ten of the components of the subtle body. Similar to how every person contains the same basic capacity for understanding and connection, these components form the common foundation of all conscious experience.

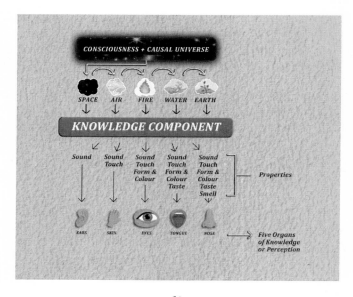

- The knowledge property first exerts itself through each of the five pure states of fundamental matter individually. **This leads to the creation of the five power centers of perception**: the subtle ear from pure space; the subtle skin from pure air; the subtle eye from pure fire; the subtle tongue from pure water; and the subtle nose from pure earth.

- Then, the knowledge property of all five states of pure matter combines **to form the five components of the inner personality**. As individual qualities combine to create the unique beauty of each person, these pure states combine to create the foundation of our inner experience.

With that, the intrinsic power of knowledge has spent itself, and **it is time for the intrinsic power of action to take over.** This leads to the formation of the remaining ten components of the subtle body.

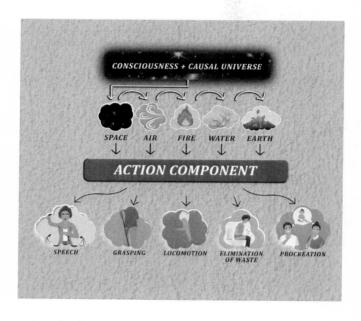

- As before, the action property first exerts itself through each of the five pure states of fundamental matter individually. **This leads to the creation of the five power centers of action:** speech from pure space; manipulation from pure air; locomotion from pure fire; elimination from pure water; and reproduction from pure earth.

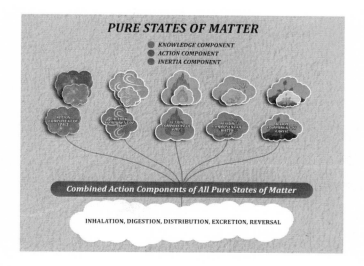

- Then, the action property of all five states of pure matter combines **to form the five power centers of physical function**.

As these two stages are unfolding, the subtle bodies of plants and animals are also being created, although in slightly different ways.

This shared origin in pure states of matter reveals another layer of our connection to all living things. We may appear different on the surface, but our subtle bodies arose from the same source, like all human experiences arise from the same fundamental emotions and sensations.

Once both the knowledge and action properties have completed their duties, the Subtle Big Bang has come to an end. The inertia property is all that

remains; when it begins to assert itself, the Gross Big Bang begins.

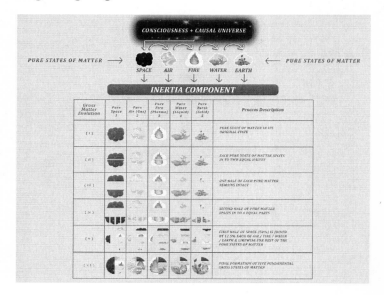

- During this event, the inertia property exerts itself through each of the five pure states of fundamental matter. This is how the five states of gross matter are created.

- However, remember that we already said it's not possible for gross matter to exist in pure form. So, as soon as these five states of matter are created, they immediately combine and blend together — much like how our individual differences combine to create the rich complexity of human relationships.

- Once this has happened, the event that most people imagine when they think of the Big Bang begins. The elements and the forces of the universe are formed—everything that will one day create the stars, planets, and life forms that we see all around us. Every atom in your body, every cell in your brain, every molecule of air you breathe—all of it comes from this same cosmic source, this same primordial mixing of pure states into physical reality.

This describes the true nature of the creation of our universe—how it really came into being, starting from the potential contained in the causal universe. One day, our universe will break up, and all its gross and subtle matter will return to their potential forms, and the causal universe will dominate again—until the next set of Big Bangs, and the next universe.

Understanding this creation story reveals something profound about our connection to each other and to all of existence. Not only do we share the same Consciousness, as we discovered in the last chapter, but our very physical forms arose from the same source. The subtle matter that forms your thoughts and feelings, the gross matter that forms your body—these are not fundamentally different from the matter that forms everyone and everything else. **We are all expressions of the same**

fundamental reality, both in our Consciousness and in our physical nature.

In this way, we can see how the creation of the universe is cyclical, just as our own lives move through cycles. And just as the gross and subtle bodies that we have in one universe can leave their mark on the next universe, our actions in this life can shape what is to come.

With that understanding in place, let's take a moment in the next chapter to put everything we've learned so far into context before moving on to talk about some of the approaches that can help us live in harmony with these deeper truths about existence— and how they can help us live more harmoniously with the people we love.

Chapter 06

Way Forward

---⋄⋄---

So far, we have probed the profound mysteries of human existence—from the unique power of our Intellect to the eternal nature of Consciousness itself. Now that we understand these deeper truths, we're ready to discover how to use this knowledge to live a more fulfilled life.

With our analysis of Human Composition, Consciousness, Creation, we now turn to methods for attaining the fourth goal discussed earlier. The goal of **Liberation or Salvation or Self-Realization or Capturing Infinity.**

By achieving this goal, the understanding of the "You in Me" essentially transpires as "All in Me" and "Me in All"

The next step is to explore the methods for achieving this state, focusing on both how and who.

Who Will Proceed?

Readers of this book generally fall into a few categories. Some will be skeptical and dismissive, while others may find value but feel they have learned enough to set it aside. A smaller group will integrate these ideas into their scientific practices, leading to advances in understanding.

The smallest segment — a rare sliver will commit to pursuing Infinity, believing that dissolving thought can lead to unity with the Infinite. While ideally all readers would pursue this objective, dedication is essential, and many will not.

Once this small group recognizes that their purpose is to pursue the Infinite, they must prepare themselves, much like the extensive preparation required for the launch of James Webb Space Telescope. This involves refining their internal instruments—ego, memory, Intellects, and Mind.

Although preparation requires seriousness, it can be guided by proven methods. Success in capturing Infinity depends on the intensity of one's desire to make this pursuit their primary goal.

Let's discuss how to prepare for this journey and the principles related to the book's content.

Science and Vedanta

In this section, we will explore concepts from Vedanta, a framework of logical tools and principles guiding the pursuit of Infinity.

All previously discussed concepts are rooted in the Philosophy of Vedanta. Initially, it wasn't mentioned due to common misconceptions associating it with mysticism, which can appear incompatible with science. However, Vedanta can be seen as an extension of scientific thought, highlighting that science and physics are derivatives of it.

This book aims to bridge the gap between science and philosophy, as Vedanta encompasses both. In the upcoming chapters, we will introduce some Sanskrit terms defined to aid your understanding in the pursuit of Infinity.

Foundations in Vedanta

Vedanta originates from the Vedas, ancient texts divided into four groups: Rig, Yajur, Saama, and Atharvana. Each concludes with the Upanishads, which discuss concepts like Consciousness, Infinity, and human goals.

"Vedanta" means "the end of knowledge," highlighting the Upanishads as the ultimate understanding of Infinity. While often associated with Hinduism, Vedanta is a secular philosophy applicable to all.

Key texts include the Upanishads, Brahma Sutras, and Bhagavad Gita, known as the 'Prasthaana Trayam.' The Upanishads are cryptic, with 108 recognized as Authentic. The Brahma Sutras organize their messages, while the Bhagavad Gita clarifies and expands them.

Studying these texts, particularly the Bhagavad Gita and a few Upanishads, along with consistent study under a teacher, is essential for those seeking a deeper understanding of Infinity.

Prerequisites

The pursuit of Infinity requires specific qualifications, much like prestigious institutions. The reader, now the seeker, surely possesses some of these qualifications, but dedicated effort over time is essential for full attainment.

The Four-Fold Qualifications

Vedanta outlines four key qualifications for pursuing Infinity, known as Sadhana Chatushtayam, meaning 'Four-Fold Qualifications'.

First Qualification: Intense Burning Desire for Infinity (Mumukshatvam)

The first requirement is a strong desire to unite with the Infinite Self, termed Mumukshatvam. This desire is connected to happiness and is essential to escape the cycle of dissatisfaction associated with impermanent goals, collectively known as "Samsaara."

To illustrate, consider being trapped underwater or in a burning house; your sole focus would be to escape. Similarly, the intense desire for Infinity is crucial for breaking free from suffering.

Even a small commitment of 5 to 10 percent of your thoughts toward this goal can lead to greater intensity over time. Achieving freedom from Samsaara, known as Moksham or Mukti, signifies unity with Infinite Consciousness, or termed as the Infinite "BRAHMAN"

"Brahman" is different from "Brahmiin," which refers to the priestly caste in India. Initially intended to help society, the caste system has become a burden. Anyone who dedicates their life to realizing the Infinite Brahman, regardless of background, can be called a Brahmiin.

Second Qualification: Discrimination (Vivekam)

Discrimination, or 'Vivekam', is the ability to think critically and differentiate between the permanent and impermanent aspects of life. It helps us recognize that while we have temporary needs for security and comfort, true happiness should not depend on fleeting achievements.

Though time, space, and causation may seem permanent, they are also impermanent. Understanding this truth relies on the strength of our Intellect.

You don't need to start with advanced discrimination. Simply trying to differentiate the lasting from the transient is a valuable first step, and this ability will grow over time, guiding you toward Infinite Consciousness.

Third Qualification: Dispassion (Vairagyam)

Dispassion, or Vairagyam, is about mastering one's sensory experiences and remaining unaffected by emotional stimuli. It does not mean escaping the sensory world, but rather focusing on a permanent goal without being distracted by temporary pleasures.

While enjoying fleeting experiences, one must recognize their impermanence. Dispassion involves valuing sensory objects and relationships to fulfill secondary goals, all while prioritizing the eternal goal of capturing Infinity.

By focusing on this highest goal, individuals can act with detachment, experiencing happiness and resilience despite setbacks. This concept is summarized by the phrase: *"Attach to the Attachment of the Detached, to get Detached from the Attached."*

Fourth Qualification: Six-Fold Wealth (Shatka Sampathi)

Shatka Sampathi, or "Six-Fold Wealth," is the inner discipline that surpasses material wealth. It requires cultivating self-discipline to interact harmoniously with the world.

1. Equanimous Mind (Samam)

"Samam" refers to a balanced Mind rather than mere self-control. It emphasizes managing desires without suppression, which can lead to stress. A strong Intellect is essential for achieving this equanimity. Future sections will address specific practices to nurture these qualities.

2. Sense Regulation (Dhamam)

In previous discussions, we noted how the five sensory organs are continuously engaged with the external world. These organs send stimuli to the Mind during the waking state, which translates them into thoughts. Each sensory experience can generate new thoughts, leading to an overwhelming flow of ideas.

Vedanta promotes Dhamam, or the regulation of sense perceptions, as a way to filter out unnecessary sensory inputs. This practice reduces the influx of thoughts and aids in focusing on perceptions that align with one's goals.

3. Withdrawn Mind (Upa-Ramam)

The pursuit of Infinity does not eliminate secondary goals from one's life. Upa-Ramam, or mental withdrawal, helps prioritize focus on the ultimate goal by diminishing reliance on external distractions. It allows individuals to balance their attention among various activities, devoting adequate time to Infinity while still managing secondary goals.

With a withdrawn Mind, individuals concentrate on their essential duties that contribute to their objectives. Here, "introvert" means focusing on personal goals rather than seeking satisfaction from the outside world.

4. Mental Resilience (Thi-Thik-Sha)

Life is filled with varied experiences, including physical pain and emotional distress. While it is natural to seek immediate relief from such pain, new sources of discomfort will always emerge.

Enhancing mental resilience is key to coping with pain. This involves increasing one's threshold for pain and reducing identification with it, which leads to faster recovery. Strengthening resilience enables individuals to face pain in an equanimous way and accept difficult experiences.

Importantly, this does not mean being unaffected by pain or allowing harm to occur. The ability to endure pain also empowers one to set boundaries and protect against negative influences.

5. Intellectual Faith (Shraddha)

Understanding Infinity is a journey; even advanced seekers retain some ignorance. This illustrates the value of Intellectual Faith (Shraddha), which encourages an open Mind without blind acceptance. The goal is to pursue knowledge thoughtfully and without arrogance.

Two relevant quotes are:

"A belief in a thing which I do not know until I come to know what I believe in." – Joel Goldsmith

"Faith is the bird that feels the light and sings when the dawn is still dark." – Tagore

Intellectual faith accelerates the understanding of Vedantic principles.

6. Tranquil Mind/Concentration (Samaa-Dhaanam / Dhaarana)

Concentration is vital in both management and personal growth. It involves focusing the Intellect on the present task, avoiding distractions. Clear goals and milestones are necessary for effective concentration.

Objectivity supports concentration, applying Intellect consistently across life.

In summary, this section wraps up the sixth aspect of inner wealth, leading into upcoming chapters on methods for pursuing Infinity.

Looking Forward

To achieve Infinity, focus on the qualifications outlined using a systematic approach. Readers likely already possess some of these qualities, including a reasonably strong Intellect.

The human personality consists of multiple layers—mental, active, and physical—each contributing to individuality. Vedanta offers guidance through various Yogas, tailored to each person's unique traits.

While often associated with exercise and Meditation, Yoga has become commercialized. In the following chapters, we will explore the true nature of various Yogas and their connection to the caste system.

Chapter 07

Blessing Turned Curse!

———— ❦❧ ————

The caste system was intended as a social justice framework to help individuals achieve human goals and equal opportunity for all to attain Infinite Consciousness. However, it has devolved into a rigid hierarchy that fosters division and bias based on birth.

In this chapter, we'll examine the societal caste system (Varna Dharmam) and the individual lifestyle system (Aashrama Dharmam), discussing their original intent versus their current state. Understanding this system is not essential for capturing Infinity, but provides vital context.

Ultimately, the same texts that outline pathways to liberation have also been used to justify oppression. To grasp this complexity, we must explore the caste system in its original context.

The Origin and Purpose of the Caste System

Human goals can be categorized into four types:

1. Security: Basics like food and shelter (Artham).

2. Comfort: Material luxuries (Kaamam).

3. Invisible Wealth: Good deeds for future rewards (Dharmam/Punnyam).

4. Infinity: Merging with ultimate Consciousness (Moksham).

Moksham / Liberation / Salvation / Infinity must be the primary goal of all humans, and along with the other three goals collectively termed as 'Purushaartham'. The means to achieve these goals are found in the Upanishads, part of the Vedas, which include the 'Veda Poorvam' focused on rituals and societal betterment.

A key system within this framework is 'Varna-Ashrama', which includes:

- Varna Dharmam: Societal caste system.

- Aashrama Dharmam: Individual lifestyle focus.

Originally intended to uplift humanity, the system has been misunderstood and misused, leading to a collapse of the caste structure. Applied correctly, it could provide security, comfort, good deeds, and liberation. We will examine this system further to clarify its true intent.

Varna Dharmam – The Societal Caste System

The Indian caste system consists of four levels:

- Brahmanan: the priestly caste.

- Kshatriyan: the caste of leaders and warriors.

- Vaishyan: the caste of merchants and businesspeople.

- Shoodran: the caste of manual laborers.

Understanding the rationale behind these distinctions is essential. Vedic texts outline three categories that define the castes, emphasizing a framework to help all individuals pursue the four human goals, particularly Moksham (Salvation).

The three categories are:

- Mental temperament (Guna)

- Profession (Karma)

- Birth (Jaati)

1. Societal Classification Based on Mental Temperament (Guna)

Guna is linked to three intrinsic properties of the universe: Knowledge, Action, and Inertia, which must also essentially be intrinsic properties within all human personalities as well.

81

The types of Guna are:

1. Saatvik Guna: Knowledge-seeking temperament found in Guna Brahmanaas, who pursue Moksham and embody contemplative values.

2. Rajasik Guna: Action-oriented temperament seen in Guna Kshatriyaas, who focus on serving and protecting their community.

3. Impure Rajasik Guna: Present in Guna Vaishyaas, who are self-interested, often neglecting societal welfare for personal gain.

4. Tamasik Guna: Present in Guna Shoodraas, who are lazy, indolent, and refuse to think and live at the expense of society.

Each individual's dominant Guna determines their caste classification, shaping their personality and guiding their actions in life.

2. Societal Classification Based on Profession (Karma)

This classification system categorizes individuals according to their chosen profession. Ideally, a person's profession should align with their predominant Guna—Karma Braahmanan, Karma Kshatriyan, Karma Vaishyan, or Karma Shoodran. However, family influence, societal pressure, and personal choices can lead individuals to professions that may not suit their mental temperament.

The four professions in this system are:

- Karma Braahmanan: Individuals dedicated to studying and teaching Vedic knowledge. This requires deep understanding and specialization in Vedic texts, making it a noble profession.

- Karma Kshatriyan: Those in governmental and administrative roles, including leaders in defense, police, and business. Their focus is on serving the community, creating wealth, and promoting the greater good.

- Karma Vaishyan: Individuals engaged in private wealth creation and business for personal gain, distinguishing them from Karma Kshatriya.

- Karma Shoodran: Workers who serve the other three classes, including laborers and semi-skilled workers. Their roles are primarily physical in nature.

Each profession is characterized by its unique contributions to society, regardless of how individuals arrived at those roles.

3. Societal Classification Based on Birth (Jaathi)

The classification of individuals based on birth, or Jaathi, is often the most misunderstood aspect of the caste system. It divides people into four castes:

- Jaathi Braahmanan
- Jaathi Kshatriyan
- Jaathi Vaishyan
- Jaathi Shoodran

Many believe that one's caste is solely determined by birth, a notion that contradicts Vedantic principles and disregards the other two classifications. For example, if someone born into a Braahmanan family chooses a profession akin to a Kshatriyan, uses their position only for personal gain, they embody the mixed castes of Jaathi Braahmanan, Karma Kshatriyan, and Guna Vaishyan simultaneously.

Conversely, a person born into a Shudra family who becomes a charitable business owner exemplifies Jaathi Shoodran, Karma Vaishyan, and Guna Kshatriyan.

The same person, who was born in a Shoodran family, sees value in Moksham and chooses to give up the business and take up Vedantic studies full-time, then becomes a Guna Braahmanan and Jaati Shoodran simultaneously.

The flaw in the current caste system is its rigid association *only* with birth, implying that value is determined solely by lineage. In truth, all individuals are equal by birth and profession, and there is no hierarchy or gradation.

But, there will be and must be a hierarchy/ gradation in the Caste based on mental temperament—Guna Braahmanan is superior to Guna Kshatriyan, and so forth—this temperament is not fixed; individuals can improve their Guna through effort.

One can also redefine their caste based on Karma by choosing professions aligned with their Guna. While fixed at birth, your Guna can influence your caste in future lives. Thus, caste is fluid, and everyone has the potential to change.

Originally, the Vedas and Manu-Smriti aimed to uplift society by educating individuals on recognizing and improving their Guna. However, due to selfish actions by certain unknown society of the past, the caste system's intent has been lost, leading to misconceptions that caste is solely determined by birth.

Restoring the caste system to its original glory and purpose would be a significant challenge and would require the re-establishment of the Aashrama system for individual growth. Let's briefly explore this second system before continuing our discussion of the pursuit of Infinity.

Aashrama Dharmam – The Individual Lifestyle System

The Aashrama system teaches individuals how to navigate different life stages with the aim of developing a predominant Saatvik Guna. It outlines four key stages, each representing a distinct lifestyle that helps achieve the four Purushaarthams:

1. Brahmachaarya Aashramam: The Student/ Beginner

2. Gruhastha Aashramam: The Householder/ Family

3. Vaanaprastha Aashramam: The Hermit

4. Sannyaasa Aashramam: The Renunciate

Many recognize these stages by name but may not realize they reflect complete lifestyles. The term 'Shramam' means "effort," and 'Aa-Shramam' signifies "effortless," highlighting the natural progression from one stage to the next.

Brahmachaarya Aashramam: The Lifestyle of a Student/Beginner

In Brahmachaarya Aashramam, the student receives foundational education with two primary goals: refining personality and acquiring essential skills for livelihood and independence.

Students can select vocational skills based on their innate tendencies, regardless of their caste. Furthermore, they engage in a personality refinement program aimed at transitioning from Tamasik to Rajasik to Saatvik states of Mind, choosing Moksham as their ultimate goal and cultivating devotion to their chosen deity.

Training includes Hatha Yoga, physical exercises, and Pranaayaama techniques for health and longevity. Students also learn timeless values known as Sanatana Dharmam, which remain relevant across ages.

In summary, Brahmachaarya Aashramam provides equal opportunities for students to pursue Moksham and develop their skills, preparing them for the next stage: Gruhastha Aashramam.

Gruhastha Ashramam: The Householder's Lifestyle

The second stage of life is the householder stage. After acquiring essential skills and values, a student enters marriage, where both partners earn a livelihood righteously while keeping Moksham (liberation) as their primary goal. They fulfill their needs for material wealth (Artham) and enjoy the comforts of life (Kaamam) within their means.

Householders embody an active lifestyle defined by Karma Yoga, which allows them to exhaust worldly desires righteously. This stage is crucial as it generates the material wealth needed to support the other three life stages.

Vaana-Prastha Aashramam: The Hermit's Lifestyle

The third stage is that of the hermit. After living as householders, individuals transition into a period of mental withdrawal from worldly activities, focusing on Upaasana Yoga to elevate their pure Rajasik temperament to a Saatvik temperament, preparing for the final life stage.

Sannyaasa Aashramam: The Renunciate's Lifestyle

The final stage is that of the renunciate. Through the practice of Upaasana Yoga, individuals purify their Minds and renounce worldly possessions. As renunciates (Sannyasii), they engage in Gnyaana Yoga, learning from a Guru and progressing through Shravanam (listening), Mananam (reflection), and Nidhi-Dhyaa-Sanam (contemplation) to achieve Moksham.

While the ideal outcome may not occur on the first attempt, the Aashrama system provides a structured path toward Moksham, supporting the pursuit of the other goals of life. In the next chapter, we will explore the various Yogas and their roles in the journey toward Infinity.

Chapter 08

Yoga and 'Medication!'

---·⁂·---

The title of this chapter is intentional. Many people who start Yoga and Meditation without proper guidance eventually rely on *"Medication!"* To understand why, we need to examine modern practices of Yoga and Meditation.

"Yoga" comes from the Sanskrit word 'yuj', meaning "to unite." While most people associate Yoga mainly with Hatha Yoga—focused on physical techniques—true Yoga encompasses various practices aimed at controlling the Mind, escaping suffering, and connecting with Infinite Consciousness.

The physical exercises, known as Yoga Asana, keep the body fit and flexible, preparing individuals for deeper spiritual practices. While Yoga Asana primarily benefits the body, Meditation is an advanced practice crucial for pursuing Infinity.

Between Yoga Asana and advanced Meditation lie several intermediate practices: Karma Yoga, Bhakti Yoga, Upaasana Yoga, and Gnyaana Yoga. Except for Bhakti Yoga, these practices engage different layers of human personality: physical, active, mental, and Intellectual. Without understanding these stages, practitioners often lack the preparation needed for a lasting commitment to Meditation, resulting in only temporary peace.

Some individuals may attend retreats to focus on Yoga and Meditation, but once they return to daily life, their commitment usually diminishes. In an effort to sustain their practice, they may force themselves to Meditate, which can lead to negative outcomes, as true commitment requires mental readiness.

True Meditation involves focusing the Mind on a single thought—Brahman or Infinity—while under the scrutiny of the Intellect. This ability develops only through systematic practice of all Yoga forms, preparing individuals for the deep Meditation that leads to experiencing Infinity.

The essence of Yoga is about merging the individual self with Infinite Consciousness. The journey to this unity requires a well-rounded understanding of all forms of Yoga, enabling practitioners to move closer to this profound connection.

At the beginning of this chapter, we introduced the primary Yogas of Vedanta: Hatha Yoga, Karma Yoga, Bhakti Yoga, Upaasana Yoga, and Gnyaana Yoga. These Yogas address various aspects of the human personality and prepare one for Vedantic Meditation.

In addition to the primary Yogas, numerous other practices exist, such as Ashtanga, Kriya, Raja, and Kundalini Yoga, among others. However, most of these ancillaries are derivative and not essential for pursuing Infinity, so we will focus on the five fundamental Yogas.

Hatha Yoga involves physical exercises and breathing techniques that promote a healthy body and prolong life, enabling the opportunity to capture Infinity. While maintaining physical fitness is important, overemphasis on the gross body can lead to neglecting the subtle body and potentially harmful behaviors like anorexia, which can shorten lifespan and hinder spiritual progress.

Adopting a vegan lifestyle, while well-intentioned, can also result in distress for others if pursued without consideration of its broader effects. Vedanta views hunger as a Divine Disease (Vaishvanara), with food serving as a temporary remedy; thus, consumption should focus on nourishment rather than obsession.

Some individuals downplay the importance of physical fitness, neglecting their gross bodies in favor of Intellectual pursuits in Vedanta. This neglect can impede their journey toward Infinity and possibly shorten their lifespan.

Luckily, the modern interest in Hatha Yoga has led to many resources available for learning and practice. Readers are encouraged to explore these resources to cultivate their physical Yoga practice while recognizing that Hatha Yoga serves as preparation for focusing on the remaining four primary Yogas. In subsequent chapters, we will discuss each of these Yogas in detail.

Chapter 09

Karma Yoga

———— ✽✽ ————

In today's world, karma has become commercialized, leading to a misunderstanding of its true meaning and significance in achieving Infinity. In this context, karma means "proper" or "right action," and thus, Karma Yoga refers to the Yoga of action.

Yoga consists of various practices that guide individuals toward union with Brahman, the Infinite Consciousness. Karma Yoga specifically strengthens three key prerequisites we discussed earlier:

1. Intense Burning Desire for Infinity (Mu-Muk-Shatvam)

2. Discrimination (Vivekam)

3. Dispassion (Vai-Raag-Yam)

We will explore how to enhance these prerequisites through Karma Yoga. The fourth prerequisite, Six-Fold Wealth (Shatka Sampathi), will be addressed through Upaasana Yoga in a later chapter.

The interrelation of these Yogas emphasizes the need to practice them intentionally and in combination, according to one's personality. This prepares individuals for Gnyaana Yoga, the Yoga of the Intellect, which involves a thorough study and contemplation of the self and the Infinite Consciousness. Consistent practice of Gnyaana Yoga leads to the wisdom of Brahman (Gnyaanam) and a merger with Infinity.

This structured approach has roots in ancient Vedic traditions. However, the book adapts elements from Gnyaana Yoga at the beginning of the book for two reasons: first, to connect with readers by demonstrating the commonalities between Vedanta and their scientific studies, and second, to show that many readers are already equipped to pursue Infinity.

Now, let's begin our exploration of Karma Yoga. As you understand the interrelation of the five Yogas and your own personality, these teachings will identify the specific practices that can help you pursue Infinity effectively.

The Logic and Practice of Karma Yoga

The primary aim of the five Yogas is to attain Infinity, or Moksham (liberation). While this is the ultimate goal, practicing these Yogas can also help achieve secondary goals. Some individuals may focus on these practices primarily for that purpose.

Vedanta emphasizes rational fulfillment of all human aspirations, which can be categorized into three secondary goals:

1. Goals of Security: Essential needs such as food, clothing, shelter, and health (Artham).

2. Goals of Comfort: Material comforts and luxuries (Kaamam).

3. Goals of Invisible Wealth: Actions taken for rewards in the afterlife (Dharmam/Punnyam).

The fourth goal, the ultimate pursuit for everyone, is liberation through merging with Infinite Consciousness (Moksham). Collectively, these goals are known as Purushaartham (Purusha-Artham), where "Purusha" means "human being" and "Artham" means "meaningful purpose."

While individuals naturally pursue these goals, prioritizing the fourth goal does not eliminate the others. Transitioning to this focus is a gradual process, as it represents a shift from pursuing goals to a subjective 'becoming' that involves letting go of unfulfilled desires. This change involves a significant realignment of one's thought patterns.

An Assessment of Desire

To begin this shift, start by assessing your desires to understand the different aspects of your personality. While your Intellect may prevail, it's important to address all parts of yourself. The pursuit of the fourth human goal involves confronting unfulfilled desires, regardless of their origins.

Don't worry if this task seems daunting. Just as losing weight requires a gradual change in diet and exercise, the pursuit of Infinity involves modifying both your physical and subtle bodies, which takes time and commitment.

Categorize your desires according to the layers of your personality: Intellectual, mental, active, and physical. You'll begin to notice certain desires that consistently arise, indicating your innate tendencies—referred to in Vedanta as Swa-Dharma, or "one's own nature." Ideally, your profession should align with your Swa-Dharma, and if it doesn't, seek ways to realign your career while ensuring you don't jeopardize your financial stability or personal relationships.

This alignment is crucial because, even as you focus on the pursuit of Infinity, you will retain many secondary goals. Concentrate on those that contribute to your personal development and minimize less significant ones.

Set realistic, unselfish goals based on the desires you've identified. These should ideally connect with your profession in a field that benefits humanity. An unselfish goal can be varied; it need not be singular or universal. If aligned with your innate tendencies, you can pursue multiple goals simultaneously.

Establishing unselfish goals is key to harnessing your Intellect in managing desires. Your Intellect acts as the guide, helping you prioritize higher-order goals over fleeting whims. As you progress, we will explore the Intellect's role in setting and achieving these goals.

Three Mental Temperaments and Three Actions

In the previous chapter, we introduced the three mental temperaments (Gunas)—Saatvik, Rajasik, and Tamasik—each corresponding to intrinsic properties of the universe: Knowledge, Action, and Inertia. All individuals possess elements of each temperament, but their overall personality is defined by which one predominates.

1. Saatvik Guna: Represents Knowledge.

2. Rajasik Guna: Represents Action.

3. Tamasik Guna: Represents Inertia.

Understanding the dominance of these temperaments is essential for self-assessment, helping individuals identify behavior patterns and areas for improvement.

Action Categories:

1. Unselfish Actions (Uttama Karma)

Tied to the Saatvik temperament, these actions prioritize societal welfare over personal gain. Those who perform Uttama Karma are calm and composed, making decisions based on Intellect rather than emotions. They find happiness in pursuing unselfish goals.

2. Selfish Actions (Madhyama Karma)

Associated with the Rajasik temperament, these actions focus on personal interests and materialistic benefits. While not harmful, they do not advance one's spiritual pursuit. Rajasik individuals often have turbulent Minds and act out of desires, experiencing stress and anxiety in their pursuits.

3. Unrighteous Actions (Adhama Karma)

Linked to the Tamasik temperament, these actions reflect a misguided sense of righteousness, leading individuals to harm others for selfish gain. Adhama

Karma performers lack purpose and responsibility, becoming burdensome to those around them.

These categories illustrate how temperament influences behavior and spiritual development.

Committing to Unselfish Actions

Every person has a combination of Saatvik, Rajasik, and Tamasik temperaments. However, one can reduce the influence of inferior temperaments by setting goals aligned with their Swa-Dharma, which requires unselfish actions—known as Uttama Karma. Focusing on these unselfish goals ensures you spend more time on meaningful pursuits, leaving little room for inconsequential desires, which tend to fade over time. As you develop this habit, these inferior desires will become less frequent, allowing the Sattvic temperament, associated with knowledge and Intellect, to predominate.

As your Intellect strengthens, your actions will be driven less by inferior desires. Pursuing Swa-Dharma goals fosters a sense of dispassion (Vairagyam), essential for capturing Infinity. This habit builds momentum and enhances your ability to discern between superior and inferior aspects, improving your discrimination (Vivekam), which is vital for Gnyaana Yoga.

These improvements can occur even without a direct pursuit of Infinity; while focusing on secondary goals, you still progress toward it.

Remember the formula for happiness:

% of Happiness = (Total Number of Desires Fulfilled / Total Number of Desires Entertained) x 100

By practicing Karma Yoga, you can increase the numerator (fulfilling Swa-Dharma goals) and decrease the denominator (eliminating inferior goals), leading to greater happiness and a refined personality. Upaasana Yoga can further enhance this refinement.

Continuing this practice with Brahman, or Infinity, as your goal will help you reduce egocentric desires and view the outcomes of your actions as divine gifts.

Karma Yoga is about dedicating proper actions (Arpanam) to universal laws (Eeshwaraa) and receiving their results (Karma Phalam) with the attitude of divine gifts (Eeshwara Prasaadam).

As you engage in this practice, your Mind will become purer and free of inferior desires, allowing it to work with your Intellect toward achieving human goals (Purushartham). This refinement will strengthen your desire for Infinity (Mumukshatvam) and prepare you for Gnyaana Yoga.

The Five-Fold Sacrificial Actions

In the ancient Vedic period, Vedanta introduced the Pancha Maha Yagnya, or Five-Fold Sacrificial Actions, which can still enhance modern practices of Uttama Karma. These actions are:

1. Appeal to the Infinite (Daiva Yagnya)

Acknowledge the vastness of Brahman, the Infinite Consciousness. Approach it with humility and sincerely wish for the welfare of all living beings and objects, using the power of thought rather than material offerings.

2. Homage to Ancestors (Pitru Yagnya)

Recognize your parents' and ancestors' roles in your life. Show gratitude by treating living relatives with care and performing Vedic rituals for those who have passed, honoring their contributions.

3. Devotion to Sages (Rishi Yagnya)

Revere the selfless sages who authored the Vedic texts. Embrace the duty of preserving and sharing their wisdom for future generations.

4. Social Service (Manushya Yagnya)

Engage in actions that uplift humanity. With the growing wealth disparity, promote educational initiatives to bridge the gap between the rich and poor, emphasizing basic human needs.

5. Protect the Environment (Bhuutha Yagnya)

Recognize your connection to the global ecosystem. Focus on reducing greenhouse gas emissions and consume resources mindfully to support environmental preservation.

With this overview of the Five-Fold Sacrificial Actions, we conclude our discussion on Karma Yoga. In the next chapter, we will explore Bhakti Yoga, a vital aspect of every Yoga practice.

Chapter 10

Bhakti Yoga

———— ✤ ————

Now that we have discussed Karma Yoga, we turn to Bhakti Yoga, a vital practice that, paradoxically, does not truly exist. This contradiction will become clearer as we delve deeper into this chapter and the subsequent ones.

The Logic and Practice of Bhakti Yoga

Bhakti translates to "devotion to God" or "devotion to the Infinite Brahman." Devotion resembles love—a continuous flow of thoughts directed toward an object or being, fostering a sense of oneness. Essentially, devotion is love aimed at a higher principle.

This love can also extend to deities, teachers (Gurus), nations, parents, or anyone you revere. Understanding the emotion of love will clarify the concept of devotion (Bhakti) and the meaning of Bhakti Yoga.

Gradations of Love

When you set goals in life, love plays a crucial role. You establish goals because you desire their outcomes, and you appreciate the methods that help you achieve them. Your pursuit of these goals stems from self-love, driving you to seek what you cherish.

However, the intensity of love differs across various aspects. Your love for the means of achieving a goal is less intense than your love for the goal itself, which, in turn, is less intense than your love for yourself. Once you reach a goal, your attachment to the means fades, and your focus shifts to new goals.

For example, recall your first relationship: the love you felt for the actions taken to bond with your partner, the depth of your feelings for that person, and how, after the relationship ended, your focus shifted to finding a new partner.

In all pursuits, there is a gradient in the intensity of love: a faint love for the means (Mandha Premam), a moderate love for the goals (Madhyama Premam), and a superior love for yourself (Utthama Premam).

Love, Devotion, and God

Different forms of love can help us understand varying intensities of devotion to God, which are influenced by how we perceive God in relation to ourselves and the Infinite.

Most people view God as a means to achieve material and emotional goals for themselves, which is termed Selfish or Dull Devotion (Mandha Bhakti). A smaller group sees God as the ultimate goal, believing that reaching Him will bring peace and happiness. While this is more admirable, Vedanta refers to it as Mediocre Devotion (Madhyama Bhakti).

Only a few individuals experience Ultimate Devotion (Utthama Bhakti), where they see God, the Infinite Brahman, as fundamentally one with themselves. At this level, devotion transcends material ends or even the goal of reaching God.

Bhakti Yoga, Which Does Not Exist

In the previous chapter, we discussed Karma Yoga, an essential discipline for achieving human goals, including Moksham, or merging with the Infinite Consciousness. Bhakti Yoga, the path of devotion, is not a standalone practice but a blend of Karma Yoga, Upaasana Yoga, and Gnyaana Yoga practiced in a devotional atmosphere.

Although the Bhagavad Gita has a chapter dedicated to Bhakti Yoga, it emphasizes that Bhakti combines the three Yogas, not a separate practice. In Karma Yoga, devotion is shown by dedicating actions to God and accepting outcomes as gifts. Likewise, Upaasana Yoga and Gnyaana Yoga are performed with the same spirit of devotion.

Thus, in all these practices, devotion is integral, and together, they form what we may call Bhakti Yoga!

Bhakti Yoga in Practice

Even without explicit Bhakti Yoga practices, certain qualities can help us recognize different levels of devotion. An individual's degree of devotion to God often reflects their understanding of God as the object of that devotion.

Vedanta defines God in three ways, based on mental temperament and Intellectual capacity:

1. Eka Roopa Eeshwara Bhakti—" devotion to God with a single form": Beginners often see God as the creator of the universe, visualizing God as a specific entity to whom they can devote themselves.

2. Aneka Roopa Eeshwara Bhakti or Vishwa Roopa Eeshwara Bhakti—" devotion to God with many forms": As one progresses, they

begin to question the source of the materials used for creation, realizing that all matter is an aspect of God, thus embracing a broader understanding of divinity.

3. Aroopa Eeshwara Bhakti—" devotion to a formless God": Further advancement leads to deeper inquiries about the existence of suffering and injustice. Vedanta clarifies that God is not just the universe but the pure Consciousness behind it, which appears as the universe's many forms.

At this level, you can worship both the formless and the various forms of God. Aroopa Bhakti includes both Eka Roopa and Aneka Roopa Bhakti.

These three levels represent the evolving nature of devotion experienced through Karma Yoga, Upaasana Yoga, and Gyaana Yoga, together comprising Bhakti Yoga.

In the next chapters, we will explore Upaasana Yoga and Gyaana Yoga, further clarifying the concept of Bhakti Yoga.

Chapter 11

Upaasana Yoga

———— ❖❖ ————

In the discussion of Karma Yoga, we emphasized the interdependence of different forms of Yoga. Practicing them deliberately and in combination is crucial, rather than just jumping to the end.

This is particularly relevant when considering the Four-Fold Qualifications. While Karma Yoga strengthens the first three prerequisites—Dispassion, Discrimination, and the Intense Burning Desire for Infinity—Upaasana Yoga addresses the fourth: Six-Fold Wealth (Shatka Sampathi), which includes:

- Equanimous Mind
- Sense Regulation
- Withdrawn Mind
- Mental Resilience

- Intellectual Faith
- Concentration

Upaasana Yoga helps cultivate these qualities, making you better equipped to pursue the four human goals (Purushaartham), especially the ultimate goal of merging with Infinity (Brahman).

Mental fitness is crucial on this path. Many people accept constant mental agitation and stress as normal. Upaasana Yoga serves as a deconditioning exercise that refines one's entire personality for more efficient goal pursuit.

Prerequisites for Practicing Upaasana Yoga

Effective Yoga practice requires both the Gross and Subtle Body to be awake and functional. While Upaasana Yoga mainly focuses on refining the Subtle Body, the health of the Gross Body is also important, as it is an extension of the Subtle Body.

We won't discuss specific physical fitness routines here, but practices like Hatha Yoga and Pranaayaama can help refine the Gross Body.

A significant prerequisite before engaging in Upaasana Yoga is refining your speech, known as verbal deconditioning or austerity of speech (Vaak-Tapas). This involves avoiding harm with your words and promoting goodwill.

As the Tamil text Thiru-Kural suggests, "A wound from fire may heal, but a wound from cruel words lingers." Verbal abuse should be minimized for mental peace. While strong words may sometimes be necessary, it is important to develop methods to communicate effectively without resorting to harmful language.

Avoiding harmful speech is not enough; cultivate pleasant, polite, and engaging speech. Ultimately, your pursuit is for Brahman, the Absolute Truth, which can only be reached through a commitment to Relative Truth—striving to avoid lies.

As you refine your Mind, you'll become sensitive to dishonesty and its effects. Achievements gained through lies will cause agitation, while those gained through truth will bring happiness. In exceptional cases, where a lie may serve a noble cause, compensatory deeds (Praaya-Chittam) may be necessary to balance its impact.

By refining your speech to align with these guidelines, you will take an important step toward deconditioning yourself and establishing your practice of Upaasana Yoga.

Before we explore Upaasana Yoga's logic and practice, it's crucial to reiterate a key point. Various methods and terms have been introduced without detailed explanations, as the main goal of this book is to familiarize you with these concepts rather than delve into extensive discussions about every idea. For further exploration, the final chapter provides an email for additional references and recommendations related to Vedanta.

The Logic and Practice of Upaasana Yoga

Refining the Mind begins with maintaining a healthy body and practicing verbal discipline, both essential for mental development, the core purpose of Upaasana Yoga. This refinement is a means to a greater aim—the pursuit of Infinity, or Brahman.

True Meditation is the ability to focus the Mind on a single thought for an extended period while excluding all distractions. Upaasana Yoga prepares the Mind for this advanced form of Meditation.

The Meaning of Upaasana

Concentration is defined as the Intellect's ability to keep the Mind engaged in present activities. While everyone has some capacity for concentration, its duration varies among individuals and is influenced by the strength of one's Intellect. Upaasana Yoga can help you gradually extend your focus and attention span.

The term Upaasana means "to sit near." It is related to "Upavaasam," meaning "to dwell."

[Note: Upaasana Yoga is often synonymous with Ashtaanga Yoga, which has become commercialized. This book will focus on Upaasana Yoga.]

So, what are we sitting or dwelling near when we practice this Yoga?

Upaasana Yoga involves using your Intellect to guide your Mind to focus on the thoughts of Brahman, the Infinite Reality. This practice helps decondition your Mind from chaos and prepares it for experiencing Infinity.

Even those with strong Intellects may struggle to maintain this focus for long periods initially. However, regardless of their Intellect, everyone can set aside a few minutes daily for these thoughts, which is the essence of Upaasana Yoga. Over time, with focused effort, your Mind will become more adept at dwelling on Brahman.

Interestingly, advanced practitioners who concentrate on Brahman for most of the day can become so absorbed that they neglect basic needs like eating. This is how 'Upavaasam' came to mean "fasting," often overshadowing its primary meaning related to Brahman.

Practicing Upaasana Yoga

To practice Upaasana Yoga, start with just five to fifteen minutes. The best time for this Meditation is early morning when your Mind is calm.

1. Choose a Quiet Space: Find a clean, secluded spot to sit comfortably with your body erect and eyes closed.

2. Withdraw Sensory Activities: Gradually disconnect from the five senses (Gnyaana Indriya Nigraham) and actions (Karma Indriya Nigraham).

3. Focus on the Present: Use your Intellect to set aside past worries and future anxieties (Mano Nigraham).

4. Practice Pranaayaama: Spend two to five minutes focusing on your breath. This will regulate your Mind and prepare you for Meditation.

Practicing Upaasana Yoga in this structured way will help increase your ability to concentrate over time.

Once you have practiced Pranaayaama for a few minutes and achieved a calm and balanced Mind, you are ready to begin Upaasana Yoga with one of the preparatory Meditations outlined below. These summaries introduce each Meditation, with a guided Meditation resource available upon request at the email provided at the end of this book.

Relaxation Meditation

The goal of Relaxation Meditation is to relax your entire being.

Begin by relaxing your physical body. Visualize each part from your head to your toes, allowing yourself to release tension. You may initially feel the weight of your body, but this will gradually become a sensation of lightness as if you have withdrawn from it completely.

As your body relaxes, notice your breathing becoming calm and regulated. Observe your inhalation and exhalation while remaining in this relaxed state.

Next, focus on relaxing your Mind. This can be challenging, as the Mind often wanders to the past or future due to stress. Stress arises from mental agitation caused by competing desires seeking immediate gratification.

In your Meditative posture, affirm that these stress-inducing desires stem from ignorance. Remind yourself that by strengthening your Intellect, you can manage these desires without needing to fulfill them immediately.

When your Mind wanders, gently guide it back to the present without self-criticism. Accept that you cannot control the past and focus on the moment, allowing the future to unfold naturally.

Visualizing a serene natural setting can enhance your relaxation. Aim for a consistent practice of Relaxation Meditation starting with five minutes, gradually increasing to ten or fifteen. Regular practice will help reduce stress and foster a relaxed state outside of Meditation.

Once you establish a consistent routine, you can continue to Concentration Meditation.

Concentration Meditation

Concentration Meditation is designed to improve your attention span. It enables you to focus on a present activity until its completion without distractions from the past or future.

There are three methods for practicing Concentration Meditation:

1. **Mental Ritual (Mental Worship):** Choose a deity from any religion and mentally perform the prescribed rituals without distractions. For example, if you follow Lord Shiva, you will sit in a Meditative posture and mentally complete the rituals associated with Shiv Maanasa Pooja.

2. **Mental Recitation:** Select a prayer lasting ten to fifteen minutes and mentally recite it from start to finish without reflecting on its meaning. This is called Maanasa Paaraayanam.

3. **Mental Chanting (Mantram)**: Choose a powerful Mantram related to Brahman, such as "Om Namah Shivaayam," and mentally chant it for ten to fifteen minutes. This practice is known as Maanasa Japam.

You can perform any of these methods individually or in sequence, helping to refine your Mind and prepare you for the next stage— Macrocosmic Meditation.

Macrocosmic Meditation

In contrast to Concentration Meditation, Macrocosmic Meditation focuses on the vast scope of the cosmos.

Begin by visualizing the universe, starting from subatomic particles, then moving to microorganisms, plants, animals, your own existence, the natural world, Earth, our Solar System, the Milky Way, nearby galaxies, and finally, the observable universe.

Recognize that Infinite Brahman pervades all of this and visualize your individuality as a tiny speck within the cosmos, which itself is a part of the Infinite Brahman.

Practicing Macrocosmic Meditation, or Vishwa Roopa Eeshwara Dhyaanam, will transform your perspective, helping you see the oneness in all beings and objects. Aim to practice this for twenty to thirty minutes daily, as it prepares you for Transformative Meditation.

Transformative Meditation

Regardless of how diligently you practice the earlier Meditations, if your inner self is burdened by negative thought patterns and desires, your efforts may be in vain. We have complex personalities, blending both good and bad traits. This awareness is unavoidable, as those with strong Intellects may find their flaws more apparent, while others may feel a nagging sense of conscience.

Transformative Meditation focuses on assessing your inner self. During this practice, identify negative traits and consciously choose to disregard them, stopping the thought flow that nourishes them. Your thoughts shape your Mind; by cutting off support to negative aspects, you can eliminate them from your personality.

Instead, Meditate on the belief that a refined, positive Mind is essential for true peace and happiness, independent of material possessions.

Thoughts have the power to shape reality, known as Sankalpa Shakti. By consistently nurturing positive thoughts and visualizing yourself as transformed, you can change your thinking patterns and gradually reshape your personality.

These four preparatory Meditations are part of Upaasana Yoga. Practicing them for just a few minutes daily can lead to Six-Fold Wealth (Shatka Sampathi), preparing you for Gnyaana Yoga.

It's important to note that there is no hierarchy between Karma Yoga and Upaasana Yoga; you don't need to complete one before starting the other. Ideally, you should establish a practice in both before exploring Gnyaana Yoga, but it's also acceptable to begin Gnyaana Yoga while progressing in the other two.

Chapter 12

Gnyaana Yoga

———❦❦———

After establishing a disciplined practice of Karma Yoga and Upaasana Yoga, you are ready to embrace Gnyaana Yoga—the Path of Knowledge.

Gnyaana Yoga is a rigorous method for attaining Knowledge of the Infinite Brahman, or Knowledge of the Self, which leads to Moksham, the fourth human goal, granting freedom from dependence on worldly beings and objects. These dependencies stem from the first three goals—physical security, material comfort, and invisible wealth—which, being tied to the external world, inherently involve suffering and a sense of incompleteness.

By achieving Moksham, you become one with Infinite Brahman and reach a state unaffected by external circumstances. You will learn to accept unchangeable situations without fear and act effectively in areas of your life that require change, guided by a strong Intellect.

The Logic and Practice of Gnyaana Yoga

To gain Knowledge of the Self—Infinite Consciousness—you need a source of knowledge (Pramaanam). For objective knowledge, we rely on:

• Sensory perceptions—our primary source.

• Inferences—our secondary source.

While perception and inference provide valuable knowledge about the universe, they cannot directly reveal the Self—the Pure Consciousness within. For that, you need the Vedantic Scriptures, including the Bhagavad Gita, Upanishads, and Brahma Sutras as a source of Knowledge.

Gnyaana Yoga in Practice

Studying these scriptures systematically is essential to acquiring Knowledge of the Self, known as Gnyaana Yoga. It consists of three stages:

• **Shravanam:** Learning the Vedantic Scriptures.

• **Mananam:** Reflecting on the Vedantic Scriptures.

• **Nidhi-Dhyaa-Sanam:** Vedantic Meditation.

In Shravanam, understanding the Vedantic texts requires guidance from a competent teacher or Guru, similar to how a fighter pilot undergoes rigorous training under skilled instructors before becoming qualified.

Shravanam involves a systematic study of Vedantic Scriptures over an extended period under the guidance of a qualified Guru. Your Guru will provide a set study schedule, and it is important to stick to it while resisting the urge to immediately clarify any doubts you may have. Many texts are written in a conversational style and will address your questions as you progress.

While it is fine to ask questions if you are Intellectually curious, the Vedantic Scriptures will ultimately provide answers, covering essential concepts related to individual existence, the universe, God (Brahman), the relationship between all three, salvation (Moksham), and the methods for attaining Moksham.

After completing Shravanam, you will proceed to Mananam, the stage of reflection. Here, you're encouraged to think independently and apply your Intellect to clarify doubts. If needed, you can discuss these with your Guru, but primarily aim to solidify your understanding through personal reflection.

The final stage, Nidhi-Dhyaa-Sanam (Vedantic Meditation), involves assimilating the knowledge acquired through Shravanam and Mananam. This process is enhanced by previously practiced Karma Yoga and Upaasana Yoga, which help prepare the

Mind. Vedantic Meditation aligns your knowing of Vedanta with your present self, gradually freeing you from emotional conditioning and leading you to become a Gnyaana Nishtaa, firmly established in Vedantic wisdom.

The transformation from Vedantic Knowledge to Vedantic Wisdom involves several key components.

First, continue studying the Vedantic texts and limit your associations only to fellow Vedantins through a practice called Sat-Sangam. This alignment ensures that external stimuli reflect a Vedantic way of life, minimizing the chances of past conditioning resurfacing. Over time, you will stop reacting based on old habits, allowing your Intellect to become more accessible at all times—before, during, and after actions.

As your actions become guided by Vedantic teachings instead of past conditioning, you will be able to effortlessly apply this Knowledge whenever needed.

Remember the Preparatory Meditations from Upaasana Yoga? They trained your Intellect to focus your Mind during short sessions. Most of your day will center on contemplating Vedantic principles in Vedantic Meditation. With a purified Mind and Intellect, maintaining concentration will become easier, leading to a deeper alignment between them. Eventually, your thoughts will shift away from the external world, dedicating your waking life to Vedantic contemplation.

This progression involves three stages of Gnyaana Yoga: Shravanam (relying on your Guru), Mananam (using your Intellect with support), and Nidhi-Dhyaa-Sanam (becoming self-reliant). At this advanced stage, you will focus your Mind on the Infinite Brahman under the continuous observation of your Intellect, excluding all other thoughts.

What happens to your personality upon reaching this elevated state? We will discuss it in the next chapter.

Chapter 13

The "You in Me" is "You in All"

———— ❧❧ ————

This chapter explores the core premise of Vedanta philosophy, "The You in Me"—merging with Infinity. All themes in the book lead to this moment, where we will examine the transformation you undergo upon reaching this state, attainable through an advanced Meditative practice known as Nidhi-Dhyaa-Sanam, the third stage of Gnyaana Yoga.

As you engage in diligent Vedantic practice, you will increasingly immerse yourself in thoughts of the Infinite Brahman. This state, called Nithya-Anithya-Viveka-Vichaaram, refers to "constant contemplation of the Permanent, Infinite Brahman, while negating the Impermanent aspects of the World." Achieving this state enables you to merge with the Infinite.

We will reference earlier chapters on Consciousness and Creation, and returning to those concepts alongside this chapter will deepen your understanding.

Macrocosmic and Microcosmic Reflections of the Infinite

We discussed the Creation process in two phases: the Causal Universe gives rise to the Subtle Universe and Subtle Body, which then leads to the Gross Universe and Gross Body. Together, these entities form the Observable Universe, or Macrocosm (Brahmaandam). Likewise, the Causal, Subtle, and Gross Bodies combine to create the Individual, the Microcosm (Pindaandam).

The merger of the Macrocosmic Universe (Eeshwara) and the Microcosmic Individual (Jeevaa) is termed Jeevaa Eeshwara Aikyam, meaning "You Merge with the Universe," absolute wisdom of the statement, *"The You in Me, Forever..."*

Understanding the Components

The Macrocosm consists of:

- Causal Universe (Kaarana Prapancham)
- Subtle Universe (Shookshma Prapancham)
- Gross Universe (Sthoola Prapancham)

The Subtle and Gross Universes begin with the Big Bang and end with the Big Crunch or Big Rip, while the Causal Universe is timeless.

Similarly, the Microcosm comprises:

- Causal Body (Kaarana Shareeram)
- Subtle Body (Shookshma Shareeram)
- Gross Body (Sthoola Shareeram)

The Subtle and Gross Bodies follow the same cycle. Despite their differences, all six components are materially composed.

Attributes of the Attribute-less Infinite

These six components are pervaded by Consciousness. Through the subtle body, all living beings exhibit Consciousness, and inert objects express Consciousness through their mere existence. The acknowledgment of any object arises from thought, which must derive Consciousness from the original source.

Thus, these components serve as mediums for reflecting the All-Pervading, Absolute, Pure, Infinite CONSCIOUSNESS. Known as Nirguna Brahman, this Infinite Consciousness lacks attributes but appears to gain them through the six Macrocosmic and Microcosmic components.

For academic interest, Infinite Pure Consciousness is referred to as Bimba Chaitanyam, while the reflected Consciousness is termed Prathi Bimba Chaitanyam.

Infinite Consciousness is attribute-less, yet reflected Consciousness appears to have attributes. This can be compared to a carnival house of mirrors, where the same physical form is distorted into different representations without changing its true nature.

Each of the six material components of the Macrocosm and Microcosm reflects a unique distorted expression of Infinite Consciousness. Vedanta describes the Macrocosmic reflections as follows:

- Antaryaamee: Consciousness reflected through the Causal Universe.

- Hiranya-Garbhaa: Consciousness reflected through the Subtle Universe.

- Viraat: Consciousness reflected through the Gross Universe.

Together, the Causal, Subtle, and Gross Universes form Brahmaandam, the Macrocosmic Universe. *The aspect of Pure Consciousness reflected through Brahmaandam is known as Eeshwaraa.*

Microcosmic Reflections Are Described As Follows:

- Praagnya: Consciousness reflected through the Causal Body.

- Taijasaa: Consciousness reflected through the Subtle Body.

- Vishwaa: Consciousness reflected through the Gross Body.

These form Pindaandam, the Microcosmic Individual. *The aspect of Pure Consciousness reflected through Pindaandam is known as Jeevaa.*

Although Jeevaa and Eeshwara acquire attributes through reflection, Infinite Consciousness itself remains unchanging and undistorted.

Attributes of Jeevaa

The attributes of Jeevaa are generally considered inferior to those of Eeshwara due to factors such as physical limitations, external influences, and emotional susceptibilities. Collectively, these inferior attributes are called Nikrushta Guna.

Attributes of Eeshwara

In contrast, Eeshwara's attributes are seen as superior because of their all-pervasive nature and the perfect order they uphold in the universe. These superior attributes are referred to as Uthkrushta Guna.

The Infinite: The Attribute-less Attribute of the Macrocosm and Microcosm

Eeshwara embodies Superior Attributes, while Jeevaa reflects Inferior Attributes. The differences arise from the six distorting and reflecting media that influence perception.

By visualizing and removing these reflective mediums, one can recognize the Original Consciousness that remains. Jeevaa appears inferior through the Gross, Subtle, and Causal Bodies, whereas Eeshwara appears superior through the same lenses. Nevertheless, both are manifestations of the Infinite Original Consciousness, Brahman.

The perceived differences between Eeshwara and Jeevaa are superficial. When examined through their intrinsic natures, they are identical; both embody the same Infinite Consciousness.

A useful analogy is the relationship between the ocean and a wave. Though distinct, both are fundamentally water. The wave represents the Microcosmic Jeevaa, while the ocean symbolizes the Macrocosmic Eeshwara. Names and forms differ, but their essential nature is the same—water.

Merging with the Infinite

You will come to this understanding in the final stage of Gnyaana Yoga, called Nidhi-Dhyaa-Sanam. At this point, after studying Vedantic texts under a Guru and reflecting on them, you will recognize that your Jeevaa and Eeshwara share the same intrinsic nature.

Through your spiritual dedication, conviction, and recognition of Oneness with the Original, Infinite Consciousness, you will reach a state of merging with Infinity (Jeevaa Eeshwara Aikyam), becoming a Gnyaana Nishtaa—fully established in the wisdom of pure Consciousness, recognize "The You in All, Forever..."

Many chapters ago, we introduced the happiness formula while discussing the logic behind capturing Infinity. You might want to revisit that chapter as it connects with our exploration of Karma, Upaasana, and Gnyaana Yoga.

As you enhance your yogic practice, you will reduce unfulfilled desires, which will increase your happiness. Eventually, you will focus on a singular thought: capturing Infinity.

In Nidhi-Dhyaa-Sanam, you will experience total absorption in the thought of Original, Infinite Consciousness. With time, this thought will become so attenuated that it will snap, making the denominator in your happiness formula zero. At that moment, you will experience Infinite happiness and merge with Infinite Consciousness, losing your individuality and becoming one with Brahman. The entire Universe will shrink to a tiny dot within you.

Through diligent practice of Gnyaana Yoga, you attain Gnyaana Phalam, the "ultimate benefit." This Moksham consists of two parts: Jeevan Mukthi, liberation during life, and Vidhaeha Mukthi, liberation after death. Jeevan Mukthi is the realization of total salvation in this lifetime, while Vidhaeha Mukthi allows you to break the cycle of birth and death, granting eternal freedom.

Next, we will discuss the Law of Past Actions (Karma) and its implications for the Gnyaana Nishtaa—both in this lifetime and after physical death.

Chapter 14

The Never-Ending Story... Ends

---- ❀❀ ----

Your practice of Gnyaana Yoga will eventually lead to a sustained Meditative state, allowing you to merge with Infinity. At that point, you will be known as a Gnyaana Nishtaa and will achieve two types of liberation: Jeevan Mukthi, or liberation in life, and Vidhaeha Mukthi, or liberation after death.

Let's explore how these concepts interconnect with the Law of Karma, which governs the cycle of birth and death.

Life and Death of a Gnyaana Nishtaa

To understand the Law of Karma, we first need to recognize the experience of a Gnyaana Nishtaa who has captured Infinity. This achievement frees the individual from the cycle of birth and rebirth.

With this in mind, we discuss Jeevan Mukthi — liberation achieved in this lifetime.

Jeevan Mukthi: Salvation in Life

As a Jeevan Mukthaa, you achieve total independence across all levels of your being:

- Physical Level: You remain unaffected by external circumstances. Regardless of whether you live in luxury or poverty, your happiness remains constant.

- Emotional Level: External factors no longer disturb your mental balance. You maintain objectivity and equanimity amidst emotional turmoil around you.

- Intellectual Level: Criticism and attempts to dishonor you will not disrupt your composure. You embody independence (Swathanthram) and experience fulfillment (Poornathwam).

Your equanimity arises from understanding that worldly changes only affect the six Reflecting Media and are perceived by Reflected Consciousness. You have identified with the Original, Infinite Consciousness and are thus unaffected by these changes.

Once you attain Jeevan Mukthi, you will live in a state of Infinite happiness until your death, at which point you achieve Vidhaeha Mukthi.

Vidhaeha Mukthi: Freedom from Rebirth

At death, you are liberated from the cycle of rebirth, or Punar-Jenmam. This liberation is governed by the Law of Karma, which means "action."

To understand the Law of Karma and how merging with Infinity helps you transcend it, you can revisit concepts such as Invisible Wealth (Good Deeds or Punnyam) and certain principles from physics, including Newton's Laws and the Law of Conservation of Matter and Energy.

Invisible Deeds: Understanding Their Nature and Effects

Every deliberate action (Karma) you take produces two types of effects—Visible Effects (Dhrishta-Phalam) and Invisible Effects (Adhrishta-Phalam). "Dhrishta" means "visible," and "Adhrishta" means "invisible."

For example, if you engage in charitable acts like providing food or shelter, you visibly reduce your resources while improving others' well-being. These tangible changes are Dhrishta-Phalam. Simultaneously, these actions also contribute to your Invisible Wealth, known as Punnyam. Conversely, harmful actions generate negative Invisible Effects termed Paapam.

The distinction between Punnyam and Paapam relies on intentionality and conscience. While most people have an inherent sense of right and wrong, negative intentions can cloud judgment, leading to continued immoral actions.

Various belief systems offer guidelines for living, but ultimately, what matters is acting according to your convictions, as your intentions shape the Invisible Effects of your deeds.

Invisible Deeds and Rebirth

Throughout your life, you accumulate Good Deeds (Punnyams) and Bad Deeds (Paapams). These Invisible Effects may not immediately manifest, but in time, Punnyams often lead to Visible Happiness (Sukham) and Paapams to Visible Pain (Dukkham).

There is no straightforward correlation between your actions and their resulting physical manifestations. Influences can combine in unpredictable ways, and not all deeds may be realized in one lifetime. When you die, all your accumulated Invisible Deeds and unfulfilled desires return to your subtle body, ultimately leading to rebirth.

Therefore, each birth (Jenma) is a continuation of an endless cycle driven by your accumulated deeds and desires, perpetuating the cycle of Reincarnation (Punar-Jenmam) until they are resolved.

Understanding the Law of Karma

The Law of Karma explains the varied experiences of living beings and the circumstances of their birth—why some are born into wealth while others face poverty or adversity. It clarifies why disasters and diseases impact some and spare others, as well as why we coexist with animals and plants. Importantly, it shows how each individual inherits their unique mental temperament based on past experiences.

This understanding is crucial for those seeking a deeper insight into existence. The Law of Karma reveals that your personality in this life results from your actions in past lives. Thus, you alone are responsible for your current happiness or unhappiness; no external force dictates your present circumstances.

All events affect Reflecting Media and are perceived by Reflected Consciousness. This means that, while you draw on Infinite Consciousness, it is merely a witness to your actions. Those familiar with the Law of Karma recognize that each person is accountable for their situation.

Once you realize that your current state is shaped by past actions, it follows that your future depends on your actions today. However, it's essential to maintain perspective. Transforming your life won't happen overnight. For example, repainting a room requires several coats to change from red to green.

Similarly, as you begin to take positive actions, remember that your past experiences will influence your progress. Through dedicated practice of Karma Yoga, Upaasana Yoga, and Gnyaana Yoga, you can gradually overcome the legacy of your past.

Technical Definition of the Law of Karma

The Law of Karma can be defined as follows: all accumulated Punnyams (good deeds), Paapams (bad deeds), and unfulfilled desires from past lives (Jenmams) are known as Sanchitham. In each new birth, a subset of this Sanchitham emerges as Praa-Rabdham, which includes the specific Punnyams, Paapams, and desires seeking fulfillment in your current life.

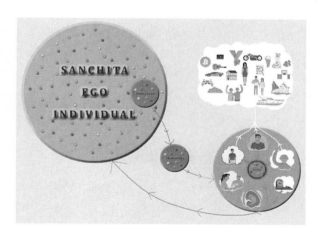

When you are born, your full Sanchitham remains in the Causal Body and does not affect your life directly; you are born only with your Praa-Rabdham. This subset determines your birth conditions—rich or poor, human, animal, or plant.

As you experience life, you deplete your Praa-Rabdham while simultaneously accumulating new Punnyams, Paapams, and desires, known as Aagaamee. Upon fully exhausting your Praa-Rabdham, which occurs at physical death, the remaining Aagaamee is added back into your Sanchitham, establishing a new Praa-Rabdham for your next life.

This cycle of Sanchitham, Praa-Rabdham, and Aagaamee drives reincarnation, bringing you into this life.

It's also worth noting that lower forms of life, such as animals and plants, are born with Praa-Rabdham but lack Intellect, preventing them from performing intentional acts. Therefore, they do not gain Aagaamee and will simply live until they exhaust their Praa-Rabdham before being reborn, hopefully as a human.

The Law of Karma in Context

Let's revisit the concept of Vidhaeha Mukthi. A deeper understanding of the Law of Karma enhances your comprehension of this principle.

Once you achieve the Meditative state known as Nidhi-Dhyaa-Sanam and merge with Infinity, you become a Gnyaana Nishtaa and attain Jeevan Mukthi—salvation in this life. This grants you ultimate knowledge of the Original, Infinite Consciousness, referred to as Brahman or God.

Gaining knowledge dispels ignorance. For example, learning physics eradicates ignorance of the subject, just as understanding the Infinite Consciousness eliminates ignorance of it.

From this, we can derive two key points. First, identification with the Reflecting Media and Reflected Consciousness stems from ignorance of the Infinite Consciousness, meaning that understanding the Infinite leads to a loss of identification with these reflections. Second, since your Sanchitham belongs to your individuality—created by the Reflecting Media and Reflected Consciousness—destroying that identification also dissolves your Sanchitham.

Even though thoughts cannot be destroyed, the combination of the Reflecting Media and Reflected Consciousness forms the Ego (Aham-Kaaram), which anchors Sanchitham. When a Jeevan Mukthaa realizes the Infinite Consciousness, the Ego dissolves, allowing the Sanchitham to merge with the Causal Universe, thus being considered "destroyed."

The Jeevan Mukthaa can no longer act with intentions and will not accumulate Aagaamee (future karma). They will still experience the fruits of past actions (Praa-Rabdham), but these experiences become insignificant as they are rooted in the Reflecting Media and Reflected Consciousness.

Ultimately, once they exhaust their Praa-Rabdham, the Jeevan Mukthaa will die and will not be reborn into a physical body (Daeham). Instead, they will achieve Vidhaeha Mukthi, liberating them from the cycle of rebirth forever.

They have brought this endless journey to a close.

Chapter 15

What Next?

-------✤✤-------

We have reached the end of our journey, covering a broad spectrum of topics: the logic behind capturing Infinity, the nuances of human composition and Consciousness, the cyclical nature of the universe, and yogic practices that can help you break free from birth and rebirth.

Now that you have gained this knowledge, you may wonder how to integrate it into your life. If you understand even a portion of these ideas, you are among the rare Intellects for whom this book was intended. To clarify your path ahead, here are three steps you can begin taking right away.

Three First Steps

1. Conduct a self-analysis to determine your mental temperament (Guna), establishing a foundation for understanding how to progress toward a Saatvik Guna.

2. Prepare your body for advanced Yoga by starting with basic Hatha Yoga and simple Pranaayaama breathing techniques.

3. Set an unselfish goal that benefits others. Focusing on this goal will reinforce your commitment to self-development and help curtail unproductive desires.

These steps will prepare you for more advanced practices like Upaasana Yoga and Gnyaana Yoga, ultimately aiding in the purification of your mind. Your objective is to bridge the gap between your knowledge and who you are, fostering resilience that connects Vedantic knowledge with wisdom.

Two Common Pitfalls

As you pursue your spiritual growth, two major challenges may arise: distractions from your five senses and your Mind. You must be prepared to recognize these pitfalls to maintain your spiritual progress.

Controlling Your Senses

Your sensory organs are constantly bombarded by external stimuli which can divert your focus. To counteract this, practice Indriya Nigraham, or the control of the senses.

Like a tortoise withdrawing into its shell when sensing danger, you should condition yourself to protect your focus by limiting the influence of distractions. However, this does not mean denying yourself sensory experiences. Enjoying these pleasures is fine, as long as they do not sidetrack your ultimate goal.

Be Mindful that many respected figures throughout history have stumbled due to a lack of control over their senses. Use your Intellect to master them and keep moving forward on your path to Infinity.

Controlling Your Mind

Your Mind is likely to be the most challenging obstacle in your pursuit of Infinity. Unlike external stimuli, you cannot escape your Mind; it is always with you. This is why practicing 'Mano Nigraham', or "control of the Mind," is essential.

When external stimuli enter your Mind, they may cause you to fixate on a person, such as a friend or loved one. At first, a few stray thoughts (Vishaya

Dhyaanam) may arise, and your Intellect must intervene to manage them. If not controlled, these thoughts can grow into admiration and attachment (Sangam), making it increasingly difficult to maintain control.

As this attachment deepens, your Mind may develop a strong desire (Kaamam) for the person, leading you to believe you cannot live without them. The desire will either be fulfilled or unfulfilled. Fulfillment may bring temporary happiness; however, your Mind will quickly seek the next desire. If unfulfilled, it can lead to anger (Krodham), retreating your Intellect, and resulting in a state of temporary madness or delusion (Samm-Moham).

Lingering in such a state can damage your personality and erode the knowledge you've gained, leading to 'Buddhi-Naasham', or "the total destruction of your Intellect." Once this occurs, your personality deteriorates (Pra-Nashyam), and you become unfit to pursue the four human goals (Purusha-Artham), losing the chance to reduce your 'Sanchitham'.

Thus, losing your Intellect disqualifies you from achieving Infinity in this life. This emphasizes the importance of keeping your Mind in check.

How to Stay on the Path to the Infinite

Reaching the end of this book indicates significant spiritual progress. After countless rebirths, you are close to capturing Infinity. Don't lose this rare chance for salvation ('Moksham') and to escape the cycle of reincarnation.

A strong Intellect is crucial for spiritual advancement. Just as you would train your body for a sport, you must daily nurture your Intellect.

To strengthen it, regularly exercise your Intellect. Question everything and validate information for yourself. This practice ensures your Intellect remains sharp, guiding you to purify your Mind and align it with your Intellect—a prerequisite for achieving Infinity.

Continue seeking new information to enhance your understanding of Vedanta. This book serves as an introduction to the vast Vedantic Scriptures, and it is recommended that you pursue additional resources.

You may opt to read the book, "Who Banged the Big Bang!", wherein the concepts discussed in this book are dealt with in depth and elaborated.

Many Vedantic institutes worldwide focus on teaching these scriptures. If you're interested, information about some of these institutes is available via email. Choose an institute that fits your location, budget, language, and learning style.

The author can offer guidance on suitable institutes and address any questions you may have, including recommendations for guided Meditation courses. Please reach out via: **life@vedantic.org**

As you finish this book, remember that the ideas here reflect teachings from various Vedantic masters. The author has rearranged some concepts for clarity, but the essence remains timeless. You are on the same journey toward Infinity.

About the Author

Prabha is a renowned meta-physicist, engineer, and entrepreneur. He has dedicated over 25 years in study and research on Causality, Creation, Infinity, Consciousness, and Self-Development. He observed that many physicists, thinkers, researchers, readers, struggle to grasp Trans-Scientific concepts. Through his contemporary and accessible explanations, Prabha simplifies these trans-scientific mysteries, making them understandable for readers of all backgrounds.

By applying simple meta-physical methodologies in his engineering business, Prabha has achieved significant material success. Prabha is convinced that anyone can embark on this transformative journey and attain extraordinary accomplishments. He lives in Dubai with his wife, Rosh, who unconditionally supports all his endeavors.

Made in United States
Cleveland, OH
26 April 2025

16430855R00088